Finally, a book on parenting that doesn't merely tell Christians how to do it, but lays a rich biblical foundation for why it matters and how it glorifies God. Striking a wonderful balance between practical advice and theological wisdom, this volume is a must-read for all parents.

Michael J. & Melissa B. Kruger
President, RTS Charlotte and author of *The Envy of Eve* (respectively)

It is with great joy that we recommend *Equipping for Life*, a parenting tool that is 'biblically based, theologically grounded, and missionally oriented.' We've known the Köstenbergers for more than 30 years and have journeyed alongside them as they've fleshed out these principles in their own lives. Written together by a father and a mother, this valuable volume couples the Köstenbergers' trademark first-rate scholarship with their hearts for training the next generation to embrace God's design for parenting and to build families on a strong biblical foundation.

Craig & Theresa Bowen
Pastor and founder of A Candle in the Window Hospitality Network (respectively)

Solomon records for us the principle that safety is found in a multitude of counselors. Andreas and Margaret Köstenberger need to be added to your circle of wise counselors. This book is practical, convicting, and heart-warming. Each principle and page is forged from personal experience and guided by biblical truth—a refreshing ble᠁ ᠁f realism from life and revelation from God.

Senioɪ

D1115339

This rich and enjoyable book rings true on every page. Avoiding clichés and simplistic formulas, it focuses on character—in parents as well as in their children. More importantly, it focuses on God, His priorities, and His parent-like attributes. In calling for parenting that is *realistic, relational,* and *responsible,* the book covers a whole gamut of issues from infancy to in-laws to education. The authors have been there, done that, and share what they have learned with tact, grace, and care. I warmly recommend this book for prospective parents, new parents, parents-in-the-trenches, and mentors of parents.

Robert W. Yarbrough
Professor of New Testament, Covenant Theological Seminary

If you are a Christian parent who believes that education is very important, but that character is even more important, then this book is for you. The Köstenbergers wrote this helpful book from the perspective of solid theology, daily practicality, and a wealth of experience. There are few books on Christian parenting that so beautifully blend the three. If you're a parent looking for guidance on raising children in a Christ-exalting, gospel-centered, biblically-faithful way in everyday life, look no further.

Don Whitney
Professor of Biblical Spirituality,
Associate Dean for the School of Theology, The Southern Baptist Theological Seminary, and author of *Family Worship* and *Spiritual Disciplines for the Christian Life*

As a father of five children, I'm always on the lookout for helpful parenting resources. Finding parenting resources is easy. Finding *helpful* resources is much more difficult. In *Equipping for Life: A Guide for New, Aspiring & Struggling Parents*, Drs. Köstenberger offer a refreshing remedy. *Equip-*

ping for Life presents exegetical and practical wisdom for constructing a biblical home and rearing children in the fear and admonition of the Lord. Every Christian parent ought to read this book.

Jason K. Allen
President of Midwestern Baptist Theological Seminary

Andreas and Margaret Köstenberger distill many years of wisdom and experience in this gold mine for parents, especially those with young children. Realistic rather than idealistic, hope-giving yet not trite, rigorously biblical yet culturally aware, no-nonsense yet light-hearted, this book will drive parents more deeply into the Bible in reverence, more deeply toward each other in unity, and more deeply toward their children in love.

Dane Ortlund
Executive Vice President and Bible Publisher, Crossway

For years I have benefitted from Dr. Köstenberger's careful and insightful scholarship. To see he and his wife devote their considerable talents to the most important of Christian duties is very exciting. I especially appreciated the emphasis on relationship and the Fatherhood of God. As believers instructed by the gospel, the Köstenbergers show us this in everything.

J. D. Greear
Lead Pastor, The Summit Church

In *Equipping for Life*, you will find an excellent resource to help you whether you are a new parent, a struggling parent, or in need of some fresh insight and encouragement. Packed with godly insights and encouragement, the Köstenbergers give us a thoroughly biblical grounding to the practicalities of parenting for the glory of Christ.

Josh Moody
Senior Pastor, College Church in Wheaton

What would it look like for two first-rate Christian scholars—who also happen to be married and have raised four children of their own—to team up to write an accessible book that is rooted in the Bible and speaks to the practicalities of parenting? We no longer need to wonder. Andreas and Margaret Köstenberger have done it. *Equipping for Life* is a first stop for new parents and an important resource for old ones.

Joshua D. Chatraw
Executive Director of the Center for Apologetics and Cultural Engagement, School of Divinity, Liberty University

ANDREAS & MARGARET KÖSTENBERGER

EQUIPPING
for LIFE

A GUIDE FOR NEW,
ASPIRING & STRUGGLING PARENTS

CONTENTS

Part 3. Responsible Parenting
Guiding your children toward responsible adulthood

LIST OF FIGURES

Acknowledgments

Wow! We're done. We're finally done! We thought writing this book would never end. But with our publisher's deadline fast approaching, it's finally time to wrap this baby up. If it weren't for breaks in parenting such as music camps, this book could never have been written, because it would have been wrong to neglect parenting to write a book about that same subject!

First, then, we'd like to express gratitude to our children.

Thank you, Lauren, for your keen sense of justice, your contempt for hypocrisy, and your brilliant mind in exploring deep questions. As our firstborn, you had to suffer through many of the mistakes we made as young, inexperienced parents. Please accept our sincere apologies for those. And yet, you've charted a very ambitious course and achieved so much in your young life, with much more to come.

Thank you, Tahlia, for your obvious love for God and others and your desire to be a godly young woman, even if that means occasionally saying 'no' or not fitting in with your peers. You've built many lasting friendships and have been a blessing to so many. The way you've consistently led Bible studies throughout your four years of college, quietly and faithfully, was truly remarkable. God will honor your persistence and your quest to be all He wants you to be.

Thank you, David, for being such a wonderful young man, mature beyond your years. No parent deserves a son like you. We are truly blessed to have you as our son! Keep up the excellent work, David, and follow hard after your Lord and Savior Jesus Christ. Your love for people, your passion for Christ, and your mercy and compassion in serving others have been a tremendous example for us and inspire us in our walk with Christ.

Thank you, Timothy, for being such a sparkling, bright child with an infectious sense of humor and a wide range of gifts—music, basketball, the list goes on and on—who constantly makes us laugh and sometimes cry because we know that one day you'll be off to college! Thanks also for editing our manuscript. That was an unexpected blessing, but we were deeply encouraged that you embraced our book so enthusiastically and wanted to be part of it and make it better.

We love all of you and are grateful for you all!

Next, we'd like to thank those who've made this a better book. John Burkett, director of the Writing Center at Southeastern Seminary: thank you for urging us to include 'more of Margaret' in our manuscript—we did! Many thanks are also due Lydia Forbes for her careful reading of the entire manuscript and for her astute comments and suggestions for improvement. She took on this assignment at short notice amid a busy schedule as a young wife and parent, and we greatly appreciate it. Thanks also to Nancy Finneran who also read the manuscript at short notice and made very insightful suggestions for improvement which we took gratefully. Thanks, Nancy, for caring so deeply about parenting, and for helping us make this a better book. And thanks for helping us think through more thoroughly the implications of God's mandate to exercise dominion for parenting and how a lack thereof will likely result in chaos, disorder, and dysfunctionality. Our daughter Tahlia, too, read the entire manuscript just prior to submission and provided wonderful feedback on many of the stories, insights, and advice contained in this book. Through her, the perspective of a twenty-two-year-old young woman is also reflected in the pages you're about to read (though of course she may not agree 100 percent with everything we say!). Most recently, my secretary Jill Cochran read the manuscript as well and provided several helpful responses.

We're also grateful for our parents who raised us and sacrificed for us in so many ways. Thank you so much, mom and dad, and Mutti und Papa, for your love and the innumerable blessings you have showered on us. Not only have you been devoted parents to us, you've also blessed our children by being kind and loving grandparents.

Above all, we want to acknowledge our deep gratitude to God Himself and to the gift of His Word to us in Scripture. When it comes to parenting, we really didn't look in any significant way to other parents to learn about what it means to be a Christian parent. We rather searched the Scriptures together in our quest to be good, God-honoring parents to our children and in them discovered much that applied to our experience with our children, especially during our early years as parents. In many ways, therefore, what you read in the pages of this book is our own personal attempt to apply the wisdom of God's Word to the challenge of parenting in this imperfect world in which we live.

Finally, we're grateful to Willie Mackenzie and Christian Focus for believing in this project and for their partnership in producing it. We're very thankful for the ministry of Christian Focus and enjoyed the privilege of visiting with Willie and his family in the Scottish Highlands and of being grateful recipients of their hospitality. (At one memorable occasion, Andreas even sported a kilt!) What an inspiring, profound Christian heritage it is that undergirds this ministry; we're very privileged to have a small part in it.

From Us to You

You may be a young couple who recently had your first baby and are asking yourselves: What have we gotten ourselves into? Or you may be going through premarital counseling and are looking forward to your life together which, you hope, will include having children. Perhaps you already have several young children and are feeling overwhelmed. Maybe you're simply looking for what you hope is another useful book on parenting, knowing there's always more to learn. You may be a single, widowed, or divorced parent who is looking for ways to be a better parent, or an experienced parent or couple who is looking for a good parenting book to use in mentoring or to give to your own adult children.

Whatever your situation, and whatever your purpose for picking up this book, we want you to know that we share a vital bond because, like you, we care deeply about parenting. We believe that being a parent is one of the greatest joys, privileges, and responsibilities with which God has entrusted us.

Sadly, however, we live in a culture that in many ways diminishes the role of a parent and the task of parenting. Often the not-so-subtle message is that a career or some other avenue of self-realization is superior to the so-called dull and dreary drudgery of changing diapers, doing the laundry, and taking your children to an endless litany of ball games, piano recitals, and dance lessons. When your child finally enters college (if they do), you're told in no uncertain terms that you're no longer needed—except, of course, to pay the bills! And even well-intentioned but misguided church leaders may urge you to give your growing child independence—or at least 'more space'—but in so doing remove you from your God-ordained significant guiding and nurturing role.

It's a terrible mistake to cut the ties between parents and children for the sake of your child's 'need' for personal independence or even for the church to do its 'necessary ministry.' Instead, youth workers and others will do well to respect the God-given design of the parent-child relationship and to strive to nurture and equip parents so they can fulfill their God-given calling as a parent. Rather than interfere with or even take over this relationship—which not only lacks humility but fails to respect the divine design—community and church leaders should challenge parents to step up to their role (unless, of course, the parent-child relationship is overly dysfunctional, whereupon ministry to the parents and equipping them for the task becomes even more vital). In these and many other ways, parents are diminished in our world today.

What a shame! The world desperately needs parents who engage in parenting that is *realistic, relational,* and *responsible* ('3R parenting')—but more on that in a moment. We need moms and dads who embrace their God-given role as parents with humility, grace, commitment, a sense of stewardship,[1] love, and a healthy dose of humor. Over the years, raising four children has brought immense joy and occasional grief. Being

> *'Nothing can compare to bringing a new life into the world and then over a couple decades nurturing that young life, by God's grace, slowly but surely into mature adulthood.'*

a parent has been exhilarating and excruciating. In the words of Charles Dickens, it has been 'the best of times' and 'the worst of times.'[2] Yet we wouldn't exchange the joy of being parents to our four children—two girls, two boys (ages 24 to 15 at the time of writing)—for anything. Nothing can compare to bringing a new life into the world and then over a couple decades nurturing that young life, by God's grace, slowly but surely into mature adulthood.

The Three 'R's' of Parenting

Well, then, let us tell you a little bit about this book. In this (hopefully) engaging and accessible volume, we seek to introduce current or prospective parents to the three 'R's' of parenting: *Realism, Relationship,* and *Responsibility.* Each of these emphases is borne out by a tension we perceive especially in young parents: between idealism and realism;

---

1   Our view of parenting is that it is a stewardship from God. See also Paul David Tripp, *Parenting: 14 Gospel Principles That Can Radically Change Your Family* (Wheaton: Crossway, 2016), 13–20, who distinguishes between 'ownership' and 'ambassadorial parenting,' the latter of which is parenting that is not possessive but performed on God's behalf. Later in the book, he lists five indications of putting one's identity in one's children rather than in Christ: (1) an undue focus on success or (2) one's reputation, (3) a desire for control, (4) an emphasis on doing rather than being, and (5) making parenting too personal (pp. 80–83).

2   See the introduction to Charles Dickens, *A Tale of Two Cities,* referring to the French Revolution.

between relationship and task orientation; and between a responsible engagement with your children and a permissive stance. Within this framework, we propose an approach to parenting that accentuates the need for realism, a focus on relationship, and taking our responsibility as parents seriously, especially during our children's most formative years.

Tension	Proper Parenting Emphases (3 'R's')	Parenting Weakness
1	Realism	Idealism
2	Relationship	Task Orientation
3	Responsibility	Permissiveness

Figure 1: Three Tensions in Parenting

Many, like us, start out their parenting journey with great hope and boundless enthusiasm, only to gradually awaken to the messy and challenging reality of life as a parent. Others feel inadequate and are unsure if they're up to the task. While bringing up children isn't easy, we believe that parents can absolutely rise to the challenge! Adopting the values and proposals we present here in a spirit of hopeful realism is sure to make a difference in raising children who aren't characterized by rebellion, foolishness, and unwise decision-making but exemplify joy and maturity in growth, eventually identifying marriage partners for life along with a personal calling.

At the outset, we'd like to ask you a simple question: *What's your goal in parenting?* Truth be told, many—even those who have been parents for many years—never take time to formulate their parenting goals or reflect on their parenting philosophy. We didn't either—at first. As a result, we do the best we can, but many of us 'fall' into parenting (as one might 'fall' in love) and probably aren't as effective as we could be if we consciously developed parenting goals and objectives. But what should our goals be and how should we seek to accomplish them? In this little book, we hope to provide a *framework* laying out God's design for parenting. In this way, you won't find yourself constantly reacting to the latest crisis or disciplinary issue but instead act out of your God-given identity and role as a parent in keeping with God's larger purpose for you in Christ.

About This Book

Now, you may wonder: Who are the authors of this book? Let us tell you a little bit about ourselves. We're not parenting experts, but parents like you. We're not professional speakers who travel the worldwide lecture circuit to talk about parenting. Nor are we professional counselors who can draw on a long case log of people who have come to them with their parenting problems. We're a mom and dad, a Christian couple, who believe in mentoring and making disciples. We love God and love the joy and the challenge of being parents. We love God's Word and what it says about marriage and the family, and we dearly love our children—not as some form of idolatry but as God's unique persons, gifts for us to cherish and to help develop for Him.

You may also ask: How is this book unique and distinctive? In short, it's written not by an individual man or woman but by a married couple—both a mom and a dad *together*—who've had the joy of raising four now-grown, thriving children. As you read this book, you'll hear both of our voices interwoven with each other—male and female, husband and wife, father and mother—in a way that reflects the partnership (and occasional struggle to move toward a unified perspective) that we believe is so vital in parenting. Also, we embrace a *biblical-theological approach*, that is, we seek the Scriptures from beginning to end to see what they can teach us about a given topic—in our case, parenting.[3] That is, our approach is not primarily sociocultural (focusing on dry family structures and traditions), psychological (dealing with emotions, honing communication skills), or counseling-oriented (addressing problems in sexual sin, drug addiction, rebellious teenagers, etc.).[4] While we touch on some of these issues along the way, they are not our *primary focus*. Instead, we seek to construct a firm *biblical foundation* for parenting, based on who God has revealed Himself to be in His Word and on the purpose for which He created us as human beings in His image—male and female, and as parents. In doing so, we hope to help parents be proactive and hope to help them avoid some of these counseling issues that typically arise in today's family.

Not that we've done a perfect job—far from it. As a matter of fact, I'm slightly embarrassed to say that *before* marriage and children, the only 'C' I got in seminary was in a course

---

3   We tried to keep this book succinct so it is useful for young couples who want to be grounded in parenting essentials. For the necessary background, see our book *God's Design for Man and Woman: A Biblical-Theological Survey* (Wheaton: Crossway, 2014), in which we explore the biblical-theological foundations of manhood and womanhood according to God's design. For a biblical foundation for marriage and the family, including chapters on singleness, divorce and remarriage, and homosexuality, as well as issues related to parenting (chaps. 7 and 8), see Andreas J. Köstenberger with David W. Jones, *God, Marriage, and Family: Rebuilding the Biblical Foundation*, 2nd ed. (Wheaton: Crossway, 2010); or more succinctly by the same authors, *Marriage and the Family: Biblical Essentials* (Wheaton: Crossway, 2012), including chap. 4 on reproduction and parenting).

4   For a principle and tradition-oriented approach to parenting in what a previous edition called 'common sense parenting,' see Kent and Barbara Hughes, *Disciplines of a Godly Family* (Wheaton: Crossway, 2007).

on parenting![5] Along the way, we've certainly made our share of mistakes. However, we've learned a few parenting lessons and have tried to make the necessary adjustments along the way. Hopefully you'll be able to do a better job than we did as you're equipped with some of the practical and biblical insights we have learned and share in this book.

> 'These parenting proposals are biblically based, theologically grounded, and missionally oriented.'

This book should also prove helpful for growing families in making the necessary adjustments to round out their parenting experience. Mentors might find this a useful tool for discussing parenting with their mentees. We want this to be a fun and practical tool that can make a difference in the lives of people who can use the input. The volume includes nine relatively short chapters in three parts, with a touch of humor to keep things light-hearted.

At the same time, *unlike* a fair share of parenting books on the market (Buyer, beware), these parenting proposals aim to be *biblically based, theologically grounded,* and *missionally oriented,* emphases that are integrally interwoven within the texture of this book. Every chapter begins with a section entitled 'What's Up?' that poses a few introductory questions based on a short reading of a relevant Bible passage intending to prepare you spiritually for the contents of the chapter. At the end of each chapter, you will find a concluding por-

---

5   It was an online course taught by the inimitable Buck Hatch at Columbia International University called 'God's Blueprint for Biblical Parenting.' Incidentally, I also took his course on marriage and did marginally better, pulling a B minus (my two worst grades in seminary). What am I doing writing this book? All I can say is, hopefully grades don't always tell the whole story of who a person really is. I believe I've learned a lot since then, so please continue reading and judge for yourself.

tion entitled 'What's Next?' aimed to be practical in nature and to facilitate discussion and integration of the practical and spiritual teaching in the chapter, useful for mentoring and counseling, as well as small group study.

Parenting with Perspective and Purpose

Primarily, we've written this book to help young couples gain *perspective* on the entire parenting process so they can parent with a coherent *purpose*.[6] While many young couples start out with lots of idealism and live largely in the present, facing the challenges as they come, much can be gained by understanding the *life cycle of parenting*: from infant to toddler, all the way to the teenage years and young adulthood.[7] Also, we want to assist young couples to develop a

> *'Rest in the fact that God is ultimately your children's perfect Parent; you're merely His instrument in your child's life.'*

parenting vision that's inspirational, comprehensive, and holistic. This will help you to fill your sails so you can fulfill God's calling for you as parents, and you'll be equipped to parent with perspective and purpose.

At the same time, don't be given to excessive worry or be unduly anxious or overwhelmed. Don't overestimate your role as parent; rest in the fact that God is ultimately your child's

---

6 Cf. Tripp, *Parenting*, 12, who also affirms the need for a big-picture approach to parenting, what he calls a 'big gospel parenting worldview.'

7 There may be some of you reading this book who are young couples still debating whether to have children or not or at least to delay having children until you are better off financially or otherwise more prepared to do so. For those of you, you may want to read the following book whose authors encourage young couples to go ahead and have children *now* rather than delaying: Steve and Candice Watters, *Start Your Family: Inspiration for Having Babies* (Chicago: Moody, 2009).

perfect Parent—you're merely His instrument in your child's life. Certain boundaries will naturally be set by the nature of the child, his or her natural inclinations, and even their individual calling from God. Every child is different, and most certainly children have minds of their own. Also, while guiding your child is important, don't be too heavy-handed. You won't want to destroy your child's individual sense of personhood and personality or get in the way of his or her personal relationship with God and the calling He has on their lives.

Ready, Set, Go!

Rather than stumbling along or moving aimlessly through the maze of the parenting landscape, we are convinced you'll benefit from parenting with purpose and perspective. To do this, we'll try to help build a *realistic* framework for parenting. You'll learn more about the importance of viewing parenting as cultivating a set of—at times messy, but infinitely rewarding—relationships: parents with God, parents with each other, parents with children, and children with God. You will hear us issue a clarion call not to abandon your children to the high winds and torrential waves of the culture! Otherwise, don't be surprised if they're spiritually tossed around or even swept aside by the currents of our times. Few assignments in life are more rewarding than helping a child develop a sense of mission, calling, and a connection with God and others in this world.

So, are you ready to join us as we explore the joy-filled lifetime journey of being a parent according to God's design? Come on then, let's get started!

Part 1
Realistic Parenting

Waking up to the real world of parenting

Introduction to Part 1

Having a baby can be a great, fun adventure. It all starts with the exhilarating discovery that you're pregnant. This exciting news is all a young couple needs to dream about starting their own family. They tell their parents and friends, and often post the good news on social media. They buy a new crib—or borrow a used one—and start decorating a room for the new arrival or wait until they know the baby's sex to choose the appropriate color scheme. Little time is spent thinking about the challenges that lie ahead. This isn't the time for realism—it's the time to dream and celebrate, especially if the couple has been planning to have a baby for a while.

Nine months later (after weeks or months of nausea, weight gain, and other possible discomfort, to be sure), the baby is finally born. A new life has come into the world! Those of us who have witnessed the event will agree that few experiences can compare with the wonder—the miracle—of seeing the birth of a baby. It could even make you believe that God exists if you didn't believe that already. The family rallies around the young couple, and shortly after the birth, mother and baby come home, perhaps to streamers and balloons and a *Welcome Home!* sign. Now it won't be long till some cute baby pictures are being posted on Facebook, and perhaps an announcement is sent to family and friends. It doesn't get any better than this. The Bible pronounces marital bliss on the two who enter marriage and become one. Now the two have become three. A married couple has become a family, and all is well.

Or is it?

The baby, it turns out, isn't always as sweet as in those initial pictures. In fact, if she's hungry or thirsty, or often for no apparent reason at all, she bursts out crying. As a young parent, of course, you try to troubleshoot as best you can and attempt to figure out what the problem is.

> *'Like other challenges, parenting can bring out both the best and the worst in us.'*

Chances are, the baby is hungry (guess 1). Or, he or she is tired and needs to sleep (guess 2). Or maybe there is gas in their tummy (guess 3). The list goes on and on. There will likely be some sleep deprivation, and many unsolved mysteries. No matter how hard you try, caring for a baby can't just be reduced to a science or a few simple steps. Welcome to the perplexing world of parenting!

Things won't always go perfectly in those first few weeks of parental 'bliss.' As a young couple, you may be able to take those early struggles in stride: You've read a few parenting books, talked to experienced parents, or even can call on a supportive network of family, friends, and a local church community. Yet the tension invariably mounts, and a gap opens—slowly but surely—between rosy-eyed idealism and rough-edged realism. Your baby may have instant reflux (as one of ours did), and you may spend the first six months of their young life struggling to feed them enough to help them thrive. Or, you may encounter other challenges that send you to the internet, the family doctor, or leave you bewildered and at a loss for what to do.

Parenting takes sacrifice.[1] You'll be called to sacrifice your sleep, your energy, your time—and good intentions are rarely enough. It'll take more than dreams of family happiness to make it through those tough spots. Those who are unaware of how complex parenting can be, and how different it is from what they imagine it to be in their ideal world, will most likely experience a measure of conflict and disillusionment because challenges are sure to come. Are you ready? Or are you already in over your head? Like other challenges, parenting can bring out both the best and the worst in us. Raising children is one of God's ways of building character in us, driving us closer to Him and to each other.

---

1   See Watters, *Start Your Family*, chapter 7.

1
Parenting Isn't Just About Children
It's about parents, too

What's Up?

As you begin this chapter, take time to reflect on the fact that parenting starts with parents. The person you are makes an enormous difference in the life of your child, because we tend to reproduce after our own kind. Also, begin to embrace the truth that the mission of parenting is given by God at creation and is also grounded in the fatherhood of God.

1. Read Genesis 1:26–28, Ephesians 5:1–2, and 1 Corinthians 11:1. What can you learn from these foundational passages about the role of the parent?
2. Read 1 Thessalonians 2:7–12. What can you learn from this passage about some distinctive roles of father and mother?

The Big Picture

What's the first thing that comes to your mind when you hear the word 'parenting'? Chances are, it's not 'parents' but 'children.' Parenting is all about children, right? It's about disciplining them, getting them to behave the way they should (or at least the way we want them to so they don't embarrass us in front of our friends and relatives); it's

> *'Parenting, properly conceived, starts with the parents.'*

about nurturing them, providing for them, protecting them, and preparing them for life. Well, *of course* parenting is about children. Without children, there'd be no parents. But at the same time, without parents there'd be no children. And what's true in the natural realm is even truer in the spiritual realm: The key to a child's physical and spiritual development lies primarily with the parents. *Thus parenting, properly conceived (pun intended), starts with the parents.*

So, that's where we'll start our exploration of parenting: with ourselves, the parents. What role do parents have in parenting? First, parents have only got themselves to 'blame' for the quandary they're in, correct? One important reason for this is the foundational principle of reproduction, which is this: *We tend to reproduce after our own kind.* Like it or not, our children often do as we *do*, not as we *say*. The best way to come close to nurturing the kinds of children we want, therefore, is *being* those kinds of people ourselves. Let's not make this too complicated.

At the same time, there's no shortcut to parenting. And the parenting process is as

> *'If you want to do your children a huge favor, pursue your relationship with God.'*

messy and complex as walking with God every day and keeping in step with the Spirit. In addition, new responsible relationships pile on top of existing ones with every child that is born. So, as we become more like Christ, and as our children become more like us, they, too, will become more like Christ (not to take away our children's individual responsibility). Or the opposite will be the case: If we *don't* follow Him, our children's character will likely deteriorate as well. We realize we're running the risk of sounding simplistic here, but all things being equal, it really *is* that simple: Like father, like son; like mother, like daughter. It's even in the Bible![1] So if you want to do your children a huge favor, pursue your relationship with God (He is of course worthy of your love and worship in His own right). This may mean getting up earlier, spending less time on social media, or playing less golf—but it'll be vital to becoming the parent God wants you to be.

Toward a Theology of Parenting

Created in God's Image

Marriage is the foundational institution on which parenting is built. God created us not only for community and for relationship, but specifically for *male-female partnership*. In this way, we're called both to enjoy each other's company and even sexual intimacy, but to our point here, we were created to participate in God's work in this world through having children! The Bible says, 'God created man in his image … male and female he created them.' And He told them, 'Be fruitful and multiply and fill the earth and subdue it.' Later, Scripture adds, 'Therefore a man shall leave his father and his mother and hold fast to his wife, and they shall become one flesh.'[2]

In a nutshell, this is God's plan for humanity. Through sexual union, and the children that are born, we partner not only with each other but also with God in reproducing new image bearers for His glory. Amazing! Children are a blessing from

---

1   Ezekiel 16:44.
2   Genesis 1:26–27; 2:24.

God, and a reward from Him,[3] not only because they are so adorable, but also, and more importantly, because in them we fulfill God's calling for us to reproduce and fill the earth with other human beings who bear His imprint and likeness. Parenting, therefore, has an important theological (God-related) dimension.

So how does this translate to parenting? A God-ward orientation invests parenting with great significance. We have the privilege of reproducing ourselves in the form of beings who, like us, bear God's image. This is truly a privilege and responsibility worth embracing. Grasp this reality and live it out! Parenting is so much more than the daily grind of keeping your children in line and getting them to the places they need to go. Bring up your children in the fear and admonition of the Lord, and be mindful of the larger God-sized purpose of glorifying Him in the way you raise them. Endure, persevere, and keep your eyes on Him.

As a Christian, keep in mind that your children are bearing the image of God and reflect His glory to the extent that they honor Him with their lives. Your mission as parents, to a significant extent, is therefore to help your children realize that at the very heart of their life's purpose is to glorify God as the unique individuals He has created them to be. Therefore, aim to instill in them their uniqueness and purpose from God. Remind them that God has fashioned them in a purposeful way and that there's no one exactly like them.

Your children have amazing, God-given po-

> *'Your mission as parents is to help your children realize that at the very heart of their life's purpose is glorifying God as the unique individuals He has created them to be.'*

---

3   Psalm 127:3–5.

tential to use everything they've been given for Him, and they need to be regularly reminded of this. Their gifting, their interests, their education, and eventually their vocation—all are specifically designed by and spring from the God who made them. Help them to live the adventure of a life aligned with God's purposes specifically for them! To the extent that we neglect to see our role as parents in this larger, God-centered perspective, we miss out on His full plan and purpose, and fail to allow God to receive the glory He so richly deserves.

Grounded in the Fatherhood of God

There's also another important dimension and privilege to parenting. Those of us who enter the joys and trials of parenting can experience more fully a dimension of the Godhead that would otherwise remain less familiar to us. We're talking about the fatherhood of God, which is the foundation for all human parenting. Consider the following affirmations in Scripture:

> For this reason I bow my knees before the Father, from whom every family in heaven and on earth is named ...[4]

Here we see that God is the source or origin of every family that exists, and parents, in procreation, enter spiritually into experiencing what it means to be creator.
And,

> we have had earthly fathers who disciplined us and we respected them. Shall we not much more be subject to the Father of spirits and live?[5]

Here we see that as fathers and mothers, we can relate to God on a deeper level because we can further enter experientially

---

4   Ephesians 3:14–15.
5   Hebrews 12:9.

into what it means to be sustainer, provider, protector, and ultimately parent.

Above all, then, the very notion of parenthood is grounded in *God* and who He is as *Creator*: He is 'the Father, from whom every family in heaven and on earth is named.' On this basis, the apostle Paul prays the following prayer for every member of the church:

> that according to the riches of his glory he may grant you to be strengthened with power through his Spirit in your inner being, so that Christ may dwell in your hearts through faith—that you, being rooted and grounded in love, may have strength to comprehend with all the saints what is the breadth and length and height and depth, and to know the love of Christ that surpasses knowledge, that you may be filled with all the fullness of God.[6]

Now, please reread this prayer one more time with your parenting in mind, realizing that Paul at the beginning of this passage invokes God as the 'Father from whom *every family*' is named, therefore we can appropriate this prayer for ourselves as parents and pray it for our children as well.

Think of it! *As parents*, we can be strengthened with God's power through His Spirit in our inner being so that Christ may dwell in our hearts through faith; and that, grounded in love, we may have strength to comprehend the profundity of God's love for us *and for our children* that is really beyond comprehension—a paradox—so that we may be filled with all the fullness of none other than God Himself! What's more, we can pray the same prayer *for our children*: that God may grant them to be strengthened through God's Spirit and to deeply know God's love for them. Parenting could

---

6   Ephesians 3:16–19.

be transformed if we were to adopt this perspective and pray this prayer for ourselves and for our children.

Now please read the second passage we touched on above regarding parenting:

> It is for discipline that you have to endure. God is treating you as sons. For what son is there whom his father does not discipline? If you are left without discipline, in which all have participated, then you are illegitimate children and not sons. Besides this, we have had earthly fathers who disciplined us and we respected them. Shall we not much more be subject to the Father of spirits and live? For they disciplined us for a short time as it seemed best to them, but he disciplines us for our good, that we may share his holiness. For the moment all discipline seems painful rather than pleasant, but later it yields the peaceful fruit of righteousness to those who have been trained by it.[7]

Again, it's obvious that we should conceive of parenting as grounded in God's own essential being and role as Father. Specifically, this realization and reality have the potential of transforming our experience and exercise of discipline on our children. God, the author asserts, disciplines His children— that is, believers—out of love. It's because of His love for us that He disciplines us the way He does. He disciplines us because He cares for us very deeply.

While in this passage, the author uses human parenting as an illustration for the way God acts as parent, He also affirms the kind of fatherly love we should have for our children. Ultimately, God's love is exemplary: We should take our cue from the way God loves and cares and disciplines. What's more, the entire analogy presupposes that there's an affinity

---

7   Hebrews 12:7–11.

in nature between God and earthly fathers—that as fathers, we reflect the way God acts as our Father.[8]

What flows from our reflection on the fatherhood of God, therefore, is that parenting isn't merely a matter of external effort and method but rather a God-reflecting approach to loving and caring for and discipling our children that can only work for *Christian* parents and fathers. It's a characteristic spiritually grounded in the new birth that all believers have experienced at conversion. Only *regenerate* parents, therefore, can experientially reproduce the kind of parenting—though never perfectly (as sinners)—that is characteristic of that exhibited by

> 'As fathers, we reflect the way God acts as our Father.'

God. This reflection on the nature of God thus allows us to see more clearly foundations for our parenting.[9]

By extension, what is said about the fatherhood of God and about the role of earthly fathers also applies to *mothers* because parenting is a stewardship given jointly to both the man and the woman, albeit with the man as the spiritual leader. Let's develop this important dimension a bit further now.

God's Order: The Man as Spiritual Leader

Apart from the fatherhood of God and the fact that we're created in God's image, there's another important foundational reality that is necessary to understand in developing our parenting philosophy and practice. This reality is the fact that, in marriage, God has appointed the man to a role of spiritual and functional leadership, and has brought the

---

8   For more on the role of fathers in disciplining their children, see the next chapter.

9   For a discussion of the importance of God's presence as a paradigm for fathers' and mothers' presence with their children as the essence of relational parenting, see chapter 5 below.

woman alongside him as a companion and compatible partner.[10]

Throughout Scripture, the man is shown as called to work and provide for his family, and to lead his family (as well as God's people, where qualified men are appointed to this role in the church).[11] The woman is shown to be called to a primary role in relation to her husband and children, one which involves devotion to making the home a nurturing and supportive environment for her family.[12] In all of this, the man and the woman together partner in 'exercising dominion,' that is, taking care of God's good creation, in large part, in and through the God-given family structure.[13]

The loving complementarity, in which the husband is a Christlike, sacrificial leader and the woman his gracious, compatible partner, is vital both for a God-honoring relationship which is in keeping with God's original vision and design but also as a basis for effective parenting.[14] In this way, a couple models a biblical male-female relationship to their children and this pattern undergirds their parenting. The family—both wife and children—look to and respect the man's role to lead and love sacrificially, and father and mother work in tandem as parents.[15]

---

10 The Bible calls this a 'suitable helper' (Genesis 2:18, 20, NASB).

11 See Genesis 2:5–9, 15–17; 3:17–19; 1 Timothy 3:4–5.

12 See Genesis 3:16, 20; 1 Timothy 2:15; 5:10, 14; Titus 2:4–5.

13 See Genesis 1:28.

14 See Ephesians 5:21–33, where wives are called to submit to their husbands as the church submits to Christ and husbands are called to love and spiritually nurture their wives as Christ loves the church and gave Himself up for her.

15 For a discussion of male and female roles in marriage, see Köstenberger with Jones, *God, Marriage, and Family*, chaps. 2 and 3 ('Marriage in the Old and New Testament') or more succinctly by the same authors, *Marriage and the Family*, chap. 1.

What's more, getting back to God's design and order means for father and mother to exercise proper dominion over their family, including their children. Not only should the man and the woman be rightly related to God and to each other, they should be rightly related to their children. In God's plan, raising children is *our* responsibility! We shouldn't farm them out for someone else to raise them. The world says: Delegate the care and education of your children to others; give them independence; send them away. God says: Exercise proper dominion as those created in my image—for my glory. Train, care, educate—be present with your children!

When a disciplinary issue arises, the husband is called upon to take the lead. When important decisions are to be made, again it is incumbent upon the husband to take initiative in leading through the decision-making process, though of course he would be remiss not to carefully consider his wife's wishes, input, and opinion on the matter. Often it will be the mother who needs to follow through on the discipline of the children when the father is at work, but even there she'll do so based on previously established principles and ultimately deferring to her husband's leadership in the Lord.[16]

In our experience, Andreas typically establishes broad parameters and gives overall direction to our family and our children. He sets the vision and exercises broad oversight. I'm integrally involved in many practical specifics, such as finding a suitable curriculum for school, identifying options for sports, music lessons, discerning needs, and so forth. That said, both of us are involved *together*; Andreas doesn't just delegate the children's education to me wholesale and remain

---

16 See Köstenberger with Jones, *God, Marriage, and Family*, chaps. 5 and 6 ('Family in the Old and New Testament') or more succinctly by the same authors, *Marriage and the Family*, chap. 2.

completely aloof from it. We're partners, and both of us stay actively engaged.

> *'In God's plan, raising children is our responsibility!'*

For the man to act as the leader, he must genuinely care and be continually involved. There's also a need for effective communication and agreement on a course of action, both in casting a vision and in specific decision-making. There may be a certain division of labor, but ultimately, we're in this together. And in the infrequent cases where we can't agree, I defer to Andreas's judgment. Most times, he is very reluctant to go against my judgment, though, because he has come to trust my instincts even where his mind might tell him otherwise.

Hopefully, this gives you a basic idea of what a marriage of complementarity might look like in practice where the husband is a maturing spiritual leader, the wife is growing to be a wise and intelligent partner, and the couple is exercising joint dominion over their children and family. We believe we allow God to work more powerfully through us when we embrace God's ordained roles and identities for us—in principle, from the heart, and in the day-to-day practical challenges of marriage and parenting.

Humanity's Rebellion at the Fall: Parents Are Sinners, Too

To be theologically grounded and oriented in our parenting, it's crucial to understand yet another aspect of what it means to be parents, and it is this: It's not only children who are sinners and thus need correction—Parents are sinners, too.[17] We're far from perfect. In fact, we're fallen and in need of redemption. In everyday life, we might suppress this

---

17 Cf. Tripp, *Parenting*, 90.

knowledge and live as if we're essentially good in our human nature and disposition, or at least attempt to do so in our own strength. We try hard to do the right thing, and to be good parents, and maybe there are even times when we seem to succeed. But is this *real* success or the dangerous *illusion* of success? Often, it may be the latter.

Remember the *reality* of what we're dealing with. As Jesus once said, without Him we can do nothing. Conversely, in Paul's words, we can do all things through Him who strengthens us.[18] Yet while Jesus and Paul didn't *specifically* apply these truths to parenting in these passages, we believe that they most definitely do, even especially so.

How does the realization that we—the parents—are sinners affect our identity and role and practice as parents? First, even though we're to imitate God in our role as parents, we're not God. We can, and will, make mistakes—plenty of them. So, when we do, we should in all reality and humility accept responsibility and apologize to our children asking for their forgiveness.[19] We should humble ourselves and not use our position to lord it over them or coerce our children. This is huge! We should encourage and nurture our children as responsible agents and decision-makers, equipping them to accept responsibility for their own actions and decisions by our own example.

It's easy to start out the day with good intentions, but it doesn't take long before our children begin to wear us down and our patience grows thin. We gradually get more and more exasperated, and may even eventually blow our fuse. That's it! We've had enough! And we feel like throwing in the towel. The problem is, as parents we can *never* throw in the

---

18 John 15:5; Philippians 4:13.

19 More on this in chapter 6 where we talk about conflict resolution in families.

towel (if we try, we'll have to pick it up again!). Running away from being a parent is never a realistic option. Even though our children may have done something wrong, we're still responsible for the way we respond. Fussing, complaining, or even yelling at our children in anger is a temptation, and when we succumb to it, we certainly owe our child a sincere apology. They, of course, will learn from this when they themselves experience their own sinful limitations.

It's extremely important as parents to be mindful of the fact that we're sinners. Parenting can be demanding and trying on a person. Especially for the mother who is home during the day with young (or teenage) children with little support, her character is being constantly refined. In view of this, it helps to acknowledge the limitations we both have as parents regarding our finite frame and specific personal weaknesses, not to mention the fact that we're sinners by nature. We should live in the light of these truths and expect that there'll be times of challenge and conflict. Try to be proactive; prepare the whole family for the likelihood of conflict.[20] We all will likely fall short in one way or another.

Restoration of God's Design for Marriage and the Family: Redemption in Christ

That's why we must work out our parenting—like our salvation—with fear and trembling.[21] We've seen how God created the man and the woman to exercise joint dominion over creation, with the man as the leader and the woman as his compatible partner. We've also seen how the Fall affected men and women not only generically but specifically in their

---

20   See chapter 6 for our 4 A's of dealing with conflict.

21   See Philippians 2:12–13.

male-female role and identities. So, how does redemption in Christ relate to our roles in marriage and family?[22]

First, in receiving forgiveness of sins, we also receive the *Holy Spirit*, and are enabled to live a new life of faith and obedient submission to the lordship of Christ. Second, we are *reconciled* to one another, and *forgiveness* is always available when we fall short. Third, redemption in Christ has not only ramifications for us as individuals or for relationships in general; it makes it possible for God's *original design* for man and woman (including parenting) to be *restored*.

No longer do the man and the woman need to blame each other or others (whether God or Satan) when things go wrong. No longer does the man need to abdicate his God-given leadership role or the woman act on her tendency to control her husband. Rather, as both are individually filled by God's Spirit, they're enabled to relate to each other as redeemed people in Christ.[23] The wife can trustingly submit to her husband in the Lord, respecting him and affirming him in his role as leader of the marriage and the family.[24]

The husband can love his wife sacrificially, caring for her and for his family selflessly and indefatigably as he was originally created to do by God.[25] There can again be pulling together, rather than being pulled apart, as the man and the woman are united as partners in exercising dominion over

---

22 For a thorough discussion of biblical manhood and womanhood using the schema 'Creation—Fall—Redemption—Consummation,' including a chapter on living out God's design, see our book *God's Design for Man and Woman*.

23 Ephesians 5:18. In the original language, this verse leads seamlessly into the section on marriage in verses 21–33 and even on parenting in 6:1–4.

24 Ephesians 5:22–24.

25 Ephesians 5:25–29.

the earth as God's representatives, specifically in their roles as father and mother as they raise and shepherd their children.

Fathers will serve as loving *providers* and *protectors* while mothers will serve as devoted *nurturers* and *partners* in parenting their children alongside their husbands. In this way, God's order will be restored in His image. Conversely, where parents, and fathers in particular, fail to exercise dominion, there'll likely be *disorder*, *disunity*, and *dysfunctionality*, if not *confusion* or even outright *chaos*.

In addition, parenting has an important trinitarian dimension—taking place in union with *Christ*, by the power of the *Spirit*, for *God's* glory—as the man and the woman bring up their children in the nurture and admonition of the Lord. Nevertheless, living according to God's original design will often involve apologies and extending forgiveness, starting with the parents. This process will prove redemptive and bring healing where there is brokenness and strife.

The Importance of Parental Unity

In conclusion, therefore, let's talk for a moment about the importance of parental unity. As mentioned, the Fall divided the man and the woman; and redemption made it possible for father and mother to be united again. This points to an important component in parenting: the *marriage*. The saying has merit that the best thing a man can do for his children is love their mother (and vice versa).[26] Time and effort invested in a marriage can vitally affect our success in parenting. I recently met with someone who confessed to me that he and his wife had had terrible

---

26 See chapter 11, 'That Marriages Do Not Thrive on Autopilot,' in Gary Chapman with Shannon Warden, *Things I Wish I'd Known Before We Became Parents* (Chicago: Northfield, 2016). On the man's role, see Richard D. Phillips, *The Masculine Mandate: God's Calling to Men* (Sanford, FL: Reformation Trust, 2010; though we don't agree with all his interpretations).

conflicts over how to best parent their oldest child from his wife's previous marriage. Hours were spent in fruitless discussion, and in the end, they still didn't reach agreement on how to enforce house rules, methods of discipline, suitable friendships and activities, and just about every aspect of parenting. Not only did that make parenting virtually impossible, it also put a severe strain on their marriage. This confession bears powerful witness to the importance of parental unity in raising children.

My wife, like most mothers, is passionate about instilling wisdom in our children. In principle, I certainly agree. In practice, however, consensus in the past has at times proved elusive. One of the important questions we worked through early on in our marriage and in beginning a family was regarding schooling. Should we send our children to a public school, a Christian private school, or school them at home? Friendships were another vital area of discussion. Which friendships should we encourage, and which ones should we discourage? What about certain movies or watching shows on television? Vacation? Should we go to the beach, especially with young and growing teenage sons when there are many scantily dressed young women putting their physical beauty on display? The list goes on and on.

It's hard enough for our children to navigate the treacherous waters in this beautiful yet fallen world; it's even harder if parents are unable to speak with one voice. As a couple, we've spent countless hours talking through various issues. We're grateful to testify, to the glory of God, that over time we've become much more united in our perspective on parenting than we've ever been. Parenting is arduous work. In fact, it's total commitment—to each other, to our children, and to God. In our case, differing views sometimes depended on differing maturity levels at the time of discussion. Other factors included different personalities, backgrounds, or in some cases personal preferences. Acknowledging these legitimate factors is sometimes hard but extremely valuable in working through differences. The time you spend in conversation with your spouse talking through parenting issues is vital. It truly is time well spent.

Please, listen to your spouse and to his or her concerns. Generally, try to trust each other's intentions—that both of you have the best interests of your children at heart—even if you're initially miles apart in what you think your children should be or do. Men, trust your wife's general intuitions. I've often found that my wife's instincts were far ahead of what I could cerebrally or rationally grasp about an issue or person. Recently, for instance, my wife and I couldn't reach our son

> *'Parenting is arduous work. In fact, it's total commitment—to each other, to our children, and to God.'*

by phone, and my wife, slightly concerned, said this was unlike him. She matter-of-factly conjectured that the phone may have fallen into the water (my son *was* on a lake outing). I quietly wondered, but hesitated to question her theory. When my son came home, we asked what had happened and my wife told him her hypothesis. My son replied, matter-of-factly, that my wife was exactly right—his phone had slipped out of his hands while having fun on the lake and fallen to the bottom. If not from this small, somewhat insignificant example, I take from many others in our life together that wives have discernment and concerns about potential influences in our child's life, and even if I can't see the relevance and deem them harmless or disagree, I typically heed her words of caution, especially since she is a wise, and spiritually mature woman. You'll be very glad if you do, too.[27]

---

27 Incidentally, there's one further stunning aspect to this story. Five days after my son lost his phone in the lake, one of his friends who

The Bottom Line

The person you are makes an enormous difference in the life of your child. So, don't take any shortcuts in this aspect of parenting. Don't believe parenting is all about your children, about taking them places, giving them experiences, managing their successes in school—their grades and their education—even their friends. Parenting is first and foremost about *you.* You have the privilege of living out God's original design for you as parents. As husband and wife, partner to bring up your children in the nurture and admonition of the Lord for *God's* glory, in *Christ,* and by the power of the *Spirit. You're the parent from whom parenting flows!* Parenting isn't just a *task* that is performed irrespective of the *person* exercising it. Think of parenting as moving organically from God to parent to child, like this:

God → Parent → Child

As parents, we'll reproduce after our own kind. We'll typically reap what we sow.[28] Therefore, we should not only pay

---

had an oxygen tank offered to dive into the pond to see if he could recover the phone. To his amazement, not long after diving into the water, his friend emerged with a triumphant grin, phone in hand. The phone, of course, was dead, but it had been in an iPhone waterproof case. When the two opened the case, they found the phone was completely dry. They charged it, and it started up and worked perfectly. What's more, my son had started a video before he dropped the phone in the water, which also remained intact, and recorded not only his zip line adventure but also the phone falling into the water and sinking onto the bottom of the lake! Then, darkness and silence, until the battery died about two hours later. You can't invent stories like that.

28 Though there may be exceptions. Proverbs 22:6, 'Train up a child in the way he should go; even when he is old he will not depart from it,' is a proverb, not a law of parenting, a principle that is generally (though not always) true. But see Daniel and Jonathan Akin, who contend that due to the lack of the word 'should' in the original

attention to the God-ordained role given to us but to our personal relationship with God and our own character. If my husband is driving carelessly, he shouldn't be surprised if his children—especially my sons—pattern their driving after his. If I'm worldly in the way I dress, or talk about other people behind their back, most likely my daughters will follow suit. Remember, children typically do as we do, regardless of what we say. So, parents, let's allow God's character transformation to start with *us*. Then we'll have plenty of time to parent our *children*, and chances are, they'll listen a lot more and turn out a lot better than if we neglect our own personal and spiritual development and approach parenting in isolation from it.

What's Next?

1. Reflect on and discuss your expectations for your family. What are your fears, hopes, and dreams, and how can you assess these considering biblical realism?

2. Considering what you've read in this chapter, do you think your expectations are realistic and biblical? How can you live out your God-ordained role as parents, mother and father?

3. What do you need to work on in your relationship with God and in your personal life to be better equipped as a parent?

Hebrew, the verse literally reads, 'Train a child *in his way*, and when he is old he will not depart from it.' In other words, if a child gets used to getting his way, this will become a pattern for the rest of his life. See Daniel L. and Jonathan Akin, 'Is "Train Up a Child" a Promise?,' in *Exalting Jesus in Proverbs*, Christ-Centered Exposition Commentary (Nashville: B&H, 2017), 133–40.

2
What Have We Gotten Ourselves Into?

What happened to the cute baby I held in my arms?

What's Up?

No matter how adorable, children are sinners, born with a sinful nature which cannot be reformed but must be redeemed. Though we love our children deeply, we should be careful not to idolize them. Read the following passages and begin to reflect on the vital role of parental discipline, encompassing both positive guidance and correction. Later, you'll read more about how fathers, in tandem with mothers, are primarily responsible for disciplining their children.

1. Read Genesis 3:1–7. What went wrong at the Fall, and why? What we can learn about life after the Fall from this passage?
2. Read Genesis 3:9–13, 16–21. How did God act as a parent in the aftermath of the Fall? What can we learn from the way in which God treated His children when they sinned?

The Big Picture

It's truly a joyful occasion when a baby is born to an exhilarated couple! Sooner or later, though, as we've already said, reality settles in. As this lovely baby grows, he or she appears to be focused almost entirely on him- or herself. As toddlers, they often refuse to share their toys. They may pout, hit, or scream when they don't get their way or may throw a tantrum. Soon, the realization becomes inescapable: Every child, no matter how adorable, is a sinner. This simple yet profound insight is vital for effective parenting: The sinful nature cannot be reformed; it must be redeemed. No amount of discipline can replace regeneration of your child.[1]

Children Are Adorable, Aren't They?

We still remember when one of our children was discovered telling lies in second grade, and their teacher called us to talk to us about a specific in-

> 'The sinful nature cannot be reformed; it must be redeemed. No amount of discipline can replace regeneration.'

cident that had occurred. Apart from feeling slightly embarrassed that *our* child was lying, not just once but apparently repeatedly, and this not just in the protection and privacy of our home but in the public arena of the school, we were puzzled: How could our child not be more truthful? After all, we had taught our children the value of honesty! Mercifully,

---

1   Paul Tripp provides a helpful study of the three parables of lost things in Luke 15 (*Parenting*, 100–106). He observes that children need a shepherd; they are prone to wander; and once they've strayed from the path, they're incapable of rescuing themselves. They are prone to self-destruction, self-deception, and, unless rescued, become a danger to themselves and others. Thus parenting, according to Tripp, is a continual rescue mission, and this rescue mission, in turn, is not primarily a matter of controlling behavior but of rescuing the heart (p. 109).

the lying turned out to be more of a phase than a permanent affliction, but God used these difficulties to impress on us the one simple fact: Our child, too, is a sinner in his or her own right! And this manifested itself not only in general terms but in concrete, wrong actions that could ultimately be traced to their sinful nature.

Yes, 'For all have sinned and fall short of the glory of God'—including that delightful little one you're holding in your arms![2] I know, you may not want to hear this, but while it may be an inconvenient truth, it is a reality nonetheless. Just as an aura of mystery and mystique surrounds a man and a woman 'falling in love,' it seems that a similar cloud of romanticism hovers over having a baby, regardless of the faith commitment of a given couple. A cognitive dissonance soon develops: We love the masterpiece of our own flesh and blood we created, but we sometimes (often?) hate the things they do and the grief (or at least inconvenience) they cause.

Theologians speak of 'original sin' (Catholics) or 'total depravity'(Protestants, especially Reformed ones, where 'total depravity' is the 'T' in 'TULIP,' the acronym for Reformed beliefs).[3] David in the Bible wrote, 'Surely I was sinful at birth, sinful from the time my mother conceived me.'[4] Like it or not, the sin of Adam and Eve in the Garden affects all of us, whether or not we think it's fair that we have to suffer for what others did centuries before us. God knows, if we'd been there, we likely would have done the same thing: disregard God's instructions and do things our way.[5]

---

2   Romans 3:23.

3   The other components are unconditional election, limited atonement, irresistible grace, and perseverance of the saints.

4   Psalm 51:5 (NIV).

5   See the account of the Fall of humanity in Genesis 3.

Children are sinners. We need to let that sink in. What this means, then, is not only that children *sin*, but that they are *born with a sinful nature*. They have an innate tendency to sin, a bent toward sinning (which, by the way, doesn't alter the fact that they're responsible for their actions, of course).[6] We can't see inside our children's hearts, but based on what we know about their sin nature, we know that pretty much everything they do will be motivated not by love for God, or love for others, but by love of self.[7] They can't say no to themselves and have little self-control in their own strength. They're little manipulators—and they're skilled at it, too! In fact, over time the child develops the art of manipulation to perfection, so much so that they've got you convinced that they love you, and do what they do, out of love for you. In return, you'll likely do everything in your power to make and keep them

> 'There's ample evidence [that children are sinners]. So why don't we start believing it and act accordingly?'

---

6   In addition, Paul Tripp speaks of the blinding effects of sin (*Parenting*, 88–90). He writes, 'Your children are not just selfish and rebellious, they are blind' (p. 88). As Tripp adds, what further compounds the problem is that, unlike in the case of physical blindness, those who are spiritually blind are oblivious to their blindness! Sinners are blind to their own sin and don't know it (p. 89; look at John 9, esp. the end of the chapter, for a biblical illustration)! Later in his book, Tripp draws 6 truths children need to know from a study of Psalm 51: (1) They need to see their sin, so they'll cry out for God's mercy; (2) they need to understand the nature of sin, so they don't minimize its danger; (3) they need to understand that their problem is not with their parents but with God; (4) they need to understand that sin is a nature problem, not a behavior problem; (5) they need to understand that since sin is a heart problem, the only solution is a new heart; and (6) they need to be taught to run to the only place of hope, the forgiving grace of God (pp. 170–177).

7   What is more, as time goes on, things will get worse. See 2 Timothy 3:2: 'people will be lovers of self.'

happy. Oh, if it were that simple. But as we all know, eventually sin rears its ugly head and destroys the happy picture.

So, don't trust all the family pictures—perfectly posed, all smiles—you see on social media. (We're obviously not suggesting you post unpleasant pictures.) Beneath the surface, though, there's frequently relational pain and a continual struggle with sin.

Alternatively, some may deny that sin even exists. Or maybe you're somewhere between these poles on the spectrum. Why do we, at times, deny the reality of sin, when plainly not all is well with humanity, including our children? And why do we think children are somehow exempt from this universal malady—sin—that plagues humanity? Not only does the *Bible* attest to this fact, there's also ample *anecdotal evidence*. So why don't we start believing it and act accordingly?

Adoring an Idol vs. Loving a Sinner

As parents, we should start out our journey with a healthy dose of realism. Otherwise, we're likely in for a major disappointment—or a series of major disappointments—and will likely not thrive as a parent, with unrealistic expectations on ourselves and our children. We may end up being too harsh in discipline or be tempted to overlook the need for correction. Rather than indulging a parental ideal of a sinless and adorable child, only to be rudely awakened to the reality that beneath the sweet smile lurks a sinner just like the rest of us, we can cultivate a more measured appreciation and love for our children that resembles God's disposition toward us. As God's Word tells us, 'God so loved the world, that he gave his only Son'; and again, 'God shows his love for us in that while we were still sinners, Christ died for us.'[8] He calls

---

8   John 3:16; Romans 5:8.

parents to do the same—love our children, knowing full well that they're sinners.

This reality—call it original sin, total depravity, or brokenness—is not merely a helpful insight, but a bedrock, foundational conviction that should undergird all our parenting efforts. Once we honestly acknowledge the reality of our children's sin, we'll realize more fully their need for consistent, loving correction. Though the merely external intervention of correction is necessary, as we've seen earlier,[9] acknowledge that by itself it will be insufficient to address the root problem, our child's sin nature. For this, we'll need the Spirit's assistance—dependence on Him to convict our child that they're sinners and to provide the means to be saved from their bent toward evil and from their tendency toward rebelliousness and disobedience. This, in turn, requires much patience, prayer, and persistence on the part of the parents.

> 'Once we honestly acknowledge the reality of our children's sin, we'll realize more fully their need for consistent, loving correction.'

The Root of the Problem

Sometimes, as parents, we just want to address the immediate problem—our child's misconduct. That's understandable, but somehow, we never get around to coming to terms with the underlying reality: the continual bent toward sin we have been talking about. How should we understand this proclivity toward evil? As the Bible puts it, 'All we like sheep have gone astray; we have turned—everyone—to his own way.'[10] Sometimes, our children don't blatantly disobey (though often they do). Instead, they may employ more subtle ways of

---

9   See the discussion of Hebrews 12 above.
10   Isaiah 53:6.

resistance. Like sheep lacking a strong hand, they meander. They drift, gradually veering off the path into precarious territory. Extrapolate this over the course of several years (if not decades), and you have wayward teenagers hardened into rebellion and then into adults that occupy a position diametrically opposite to where they should be—morally, vocationally, and spiritually.

So, then, rather than merely treating symptoms, let's get to the root of the problem. While children are small, they may or may not be able to understand the concept that they're sinners deep down inside. But as they grow, we should gradually alert them to the fact that there's something inside of them—their bent toward sin—that makes them do the things they do. They'll find within themselves the very same reality the apostle Paul describes: 'For I do not understand my own actions. For I do not do what I want, but I do the very thing I hate.'[11] What we as parents need to understand, then, is that not only does our child choose to disobey, he or she isn't truly free *not* to disobey because of his or her innate bent toward disobedience.

All too often, however, we operate in our relationship with our child on the premise that he is perfectly capable of obeying if he simply chooses to do so. The problem with this notion is that it presupposes that human nature is essentially good, or at least neutral. Some of you reading this chapter may not be convinced of the Bible's teaching regarding sin. In fact, there's a strong liberalism and romanticism in our culture that says people

> *'All too often, we operate in our relationship with our child on the premise that he is perfectly capable of obeying if he simply chooses to do so.'*

---

11 Romans 7:15; the whole discussion in verses 13–25 is worth reading and pondering.

can choose their own destiny—or at least they should be able to—unencumbered by interference from anyone else. However, this notion of a truly free person is a myth. Don't base your parenting on a utopia. You can only work within the realm of the reality that exists. You and your child will be better served to face the truth and deal with it in the end, to the point of your child recognizing and receiving the gift of salvation and the ability to live a life of holiness in dependence on the God who has provided this for all of us.

Why and How Should We Discipline Our Children?

That said, why and how should parents discipline their children?[12] In the everyday hustle and bustle of parenting, few issues are more important. And yet young couples are often at a loss—and older couples, too—as to how to administer discipline in keeping with Christian principles. As sinners (especially young ones!) and as those who are in the process of being spiritually formed and trained (Proverbs calls young people 'naïve' or 'simple')[13] we all need guidance and accountability. As parents, how do we live out the responsibility to bring up our children 'in the discipline and instruction of the Lord'?[14]

Before we turn to principles of parental discipline, notice in this regard that the primary responsibility for disciplining children rests with *fathers* as the spiritual leaders in the home who are primarily responsible for the spiritual condition of

---

12 For a helpful article on different levels of discipline, see Paul D. Wegner, 'Discipline in the Book of Proverbs: "To Spank or Not to Spank?"' *Journal of the Evangelical Theological Society* 48 (2005): 715–732, who provides many additional references to the available literature on the subject.

13 See, e.g., Proverbs 1:4, 22, 32; 7:7; 8:5; 9:4; 14:15, 18; 21:11; 22:3; 27:12.

14 Ephesians 6:4.

the family before God (though mothers are paramount in implementing and should be centrally involved working in tandem with their husband).[15] The following three major New Testament passages on this subject all directly and explicitly address fathers or represent them as primary agents of discipline:

- '*Fathers*, do not provoke your children to anger, but bring them up in the discipline and instruction of the Lord' (Eph. 6:4, emphasis added).
- '*Fathers*, do not provoke your children, lest they become discouraged' (Col. 3:21, emphasis added).
- 'It is for discipline that you have to endure. God is treating you as sons. For what son is there whom his *father* does not discipline? … we have had earthly *fathers* who disciplined us and we respected them … they disciplined us for a short time as it seemed best to them … Therefore lift your drooping hands and strengthen your weak knees' (Heb. 12:7–11, emphasis added).

> '*The primary responsibility for disciplining children rests with fathers as the spiritual leaders in the home who are primarily responsible for the spiritual condition of the family before God.*'

Therefore, fathers should be careful to live out their role as leaders in the enterprise of disciplining and directing their child's development. As you walk out the door and head out for work, you should not be delegating the discipline of the children to your wife *in toto*; you should rather plan, pray, and remain together in close partnership with your wife. Work out ways to keep in touch. Call her and call the children dur-

---

15 See the discussion of men's role as spiritual leaders in chapter 1 above.

ing the day to show you care and are involved. At the end of the day, be responsible to check and encourage everyone in the journey toward Christlikeness!

While we're at it, notice also the helpful references to the different responses our children may have to fatherly discipline in the above-cited passages: They may respond in anger,[16] become discouraged,[17] or be tempted to give up.[18] Our child's response may be signs we are overdoing it or approaching things incorrectly. Yet while discipline may seem painful and unpleasant at the time, Scripture tells us that the result will be holiness and righteousness in the lives of those who endure discipline and have been trained by it.[19]

Finally, embrace the biblical scope of discipline as framed in the passages highlighted. The Greek term for discipline is *paideia*, which is broader than mere correction or punishment. Ephesians 6:4 speaks of 'discipline *and instruction*' (emphasis added). In 2 Timothy 3:16, Paul says Scripture's purpose is '*teaching*, rebuke, correction, and *training in righteousness*' (NIV, emphasis added). Thus, we shouldn't think of discipline merely or even primarily in *negative* terms, though it doubtless involves correction. More positively, it is setting a child on a straight path, equipping them in moral formation and shaping of their character, so they will be 'complete, equipped for every good work.'[20]

How, then, can we best help our children deal with their sinful nature and the temptations they face in and from the world around them? Not that we have the definitive answer on this issue, but here are seven useful insights regarding

---

16 Ephesians 6:4.
17 Colossians 3:21.
18 Hebrews 12:12–13.
19 Hebrews 12:11, 14.
20 2 Timothy 3:17.

parental discipline adapted from *God, Marriage, and Family.*[21] Discipline should be:

1. **Consistent and predictable**: This has been a continual struggle for us. It's *hard* to be consistent in discipline, with each individual personality, among different children, over many years of parenting. And yet consistency is *so* important, because it helps reinforce in our children a proper view

> *[Discipline involves] setting a child on a straight path, equipping them in moral formation and shaping of their character, so they will be "complete, equipped for every good work."'*

toward God and their sin and what godly conduct should look like in our lives—and it aids in making sure there are no surprises along the way! One of our children would often say when being disciplined, 'But I didn't know!' There were times when this became frustrating. We would retort, 'What do you mean—You didn't know? Didn't we tell you?' Every time this happened, we resolved to be even more clear and specific about our expectations, to further delineate what our child should expect if he crossed those boundaries. Every time we tried to be evermore consistent.

It's helpful here to consider the biblical example of Eli, a spiritual leader in Israel, who didn't sufficiently or consistently guide his sons in the knowledge of the Lord or keep them

---

21 Köstenberger with Jones, *God, Marriage, and Family*, 147–149. See also Ed Moll and Tim Chester, *Gospel-centered Family: Becoming the Parents God Wants You to Be* (n.p.: Good Book Co., 2010), 40–41, who say that good discipline is calm, clear, consistent, and concentrated on the heart; and Melissa Kruger, '5 Principles for Disciplining Your Children,' May 18, 2016, https://www.thegospelcoalition.org/ article/5-principles-for-disciplining-your-children, who lists the following: (1) teach proactively rather than reactively; (2) give both consequences and rewards; (3) enforce the rules you give; (4) the method of discipline must be effective; and (5) catch them doing right.

accountable. As a result, his sons didn't believe in God or serve Him.[22]

To keep parental discipline in proper balance, however, note the scriptural contrast made with the godly young Samuel following the description of Eli's wayward sons. Samuel, who likely had little parental discipline to shape him, was soon 'growing in stature and in favor with the LORD and with men,'[23] having been dedicated to the Lord. God works here in ways beyond our comprehension, as in the case of Hannah, a formerly barren woman, who committed her child to the Lord for His purposes, realizing this child was not her own in the first place. Despite the fact that he grew up without parents to discipline and guide him, he became a true servant of God.[24]

2. Age-appropriate: It may seem obvious, but while discipline should be consistent, the form of discipline will likely change depending on the age of the child or young person. While you may choose to physically discipline

---

22 In 1 Samuel 2:23–25, Eli tepidly tells his sons, 'Why do you do such things, the evil things that I hear from all these people? No, my sons; for the report is not good which I hear …' (NASB). Notice that Eli repeatedly refers to things he is 'hearing' from others; whatever happened to his personal involvement and responsibility as a father? The narrator adds, 'But they would not listen to the voice of their father.' It's a sad, sad story and warning to all fathers and professional ministers that lack of parental involvement will likely lead to children who lack proper discipline and as a result have little or no regard for the things of God (vv. 12–17), engaging in sexual or other sin (v. 22).

23 1 Samuel 2:26 (NASB); cf. 1:11, 26–28.

24 Samuel had a unique role in salvation history, anointing the first two kings of Israel, Saul and David, and it wasn't a result of parental discipline that he was shaped for such a prominent spiritual role. Sadly, however, Samuel was apparently not a good father himself. At the end of his life, he appointed his sons as judges to succeed him, but we're told that 'his sons did not walk in his ways but turned aside after gain. They took bribes and perverted justice' (1 Sam. 8:3).

a small child (in love, not anger; see below), or use time-out or loss of privilege for children a little older yet still young, parenting older children will typically involve more reasoning and interaction (though loss of privilege will still be appropriate—no new basketball shoes or no use of the family car!). The important lesson here is that while we need to encourage a mindset of consistent accountability and discipline, the way we exercise these will need to grow with and adapt to our children as they grow older.

3. Fair and just: The goal of discipline is not to punish the child! That's part of the process, but the greater purpose is to point the way toward restoration and godliness, helping them to be aware of their sin, and to keep them accountable for it. In entering a relational encounter of disciplining your

> *'The goal of discipline is not to punish the child!'*

child, try to keep the perspective of your role as a responsible steward of the Lord. Make certain that the 'punishment fits the crime.' Think of Adam and Eve in the Garden and how God related to them after their sin. Both were disciplined in keeping with their transgression: the man who had been given the responsibility to tend the Garden had his work made more difficult; the woman who had been assigned the role to help her husband and to bear children was affected according to her wrongdoing: she was afflicted with a tendency to control her husband and with pain in childbearing.

'But it isn't fair!' is a perennial favorite in many families when a child is disciplined. And there may be times when a child has a point—perhaps we haven't been consistent or have leveled a punishment that was too harsh (though children rarely complain when the discipline has been too lenient!). In any case, the craving for fairness is God-given and right, and we should try to be fair (though still merciful, because our

God is very compassionate). Here, our parental credibility is at stake: If we overreact at first and then reduce the punishment and do this often, our children won't take us seriously after a while. As also mentioned, the Bible repeatedly tells parents not to be too harsh with their children or to discourage or exasperate them.[25] Remember too that we should have no favorites, or even be open to the charge of favoritism.

4. Child-specific: At the same time, it is equally true that when it comes to discipline, what may work with one child may not work equally well with another. This is because God made each child unique. Some children are more sensitive to discipline while others are more intransigent. Some are more compliant while others tend to be more independent-minded. Parental wisdom is required in balancing the need for fairness with the need for child-specific discipline that will be most effective in achieving the desired purpose. Our goals include setting proper boundaries, developing character, and teaching children that there are consequences for their actions.

5. Administered in love, not anger: It goes without saying that discipline should be administered in love, not anger. Of course, this is easier said than done, at least when annoying behavior has built up frustration and resentment over time. Keep in mind that when your child disobeys you, the ultimate problem isn't so much that you've been affronted but that God has been disregarded and offended. Our goal in parenting is to be an instrument in bringing our children under the authority of God. Parenting is a sacred trust and stewardship. Any offense to you the parent is minor compared to the responsibility that is ours to guide them to love and respect God. There are times when we may discipline our

---

25 Ephesians 6:4; Colossians 3:21.

child in anger and need to apologize to them later. We have found that it helps if when one of us has any resentment, or anger, we do our best to let the other handle the situation. If you are by yourself (spouse at work or out or you are a single parent) you can always ask your child to cool down in their room for 10-15 minutes to give a chance for you to calm down first before addressing unruly behavior. It doesn't help to complicate matters by distracting attention from the actual problem because a parent is unable to handle their own irritations.

6. Future-oriented and forward-looking: In administering discipline, we don't want to be past-oriented (What just happened?), because we can't change the past. We don't want to be stuck in the present (Will our child ever learn? What have I done wrong as a parent?). Rather, we should adopt a forward-looking point of view which focuses on our children's growth in character and on God's work in their lives and learning to parent according to this end.[26] Our hope is not found in self-effort but in spiritual transformation through God's Word and His Holy Spirit both in our lives and in the children. Seen in that light, any one small infraction is not that big a deal in and of itself but can serve as an occasion to teach our children vital lessons about life and their relationship with God and others.

7. Part of the parent-child relationship: This last point may be the most important in the context of the type of realistic, relational, and responsible approach to parenting that

> *'Parenting is more of a ministry than it is a task.'*

we advocate in this book. Discipline is part of our *relationship* with our child. Our children are works-in-progress, they

---

26 Cf. Proverbs 22:6; Hebrews 12:11.

Number	Principle of Parental Discipline	Explanation/Rationale
1	Consistent and predictable	Same offense, same punishment; know what the punishment is
2	Age-appropriate	Will look different for elementary school child than teenager
3	Fair and just	Punishment fit the 'crime'; not too harsh
4	Child-specific	Tailored to personality of individual child
5	Administered in love, not anger	Avoid annoyed or unduly personal reaction, convey a sense of love
6	Future-oriented and forward-looking	Not focused on past offense or current crisis but on desired result
7	Part of the parent-child relationship	Respect and dignity as part of relational parenting approach

Figure 2: Seven Principles of Parental Discipline

are human beings who struggle with sin and selfishness and insecurity just like we still do. We should not condemn them; they desperately need our help and understanding and partnership in this delicate, delightful venture of growing up to become a man or woman of God. What a privilege it is to be a part of God's work in the life of another precious human being—the children with whom He has entrusted us.

Some Practical Application Points

So how do we practically recognize and live out our parenting responsibilities in view of these principles? There are many implications, but here are a few ideas to get you started. As you begin to go about your days with your children, offer your children and your service as a parent to God. Submit yourself to all that He has for your children, and to the role you have in their lives. Always be prayerful. Recognize your own limitations, and the stewardship from God that parenting represents. Focus on an approach to your children that will encourage spiritual flourishing and realize that parenting is more of a ministry than it is a task.

Recognizing your children's spiritual limitations—that they're sinners and no better or worse than other children in the neighborhood or at church—will be helpful. God has created your children for *His purposes*. Stay close to the Lord and follow His leading, renouncing personal pride and any undue self-importance you may harbor regarding even your children's achievements. Are they the first to walk in the nursery? Or the first to say a word in a mother-child group? Are they maybe the earliest to be potty-trained? Parents compete about the most *trivial* things. Other debates of more concern surround parenting methods, such as organic vs. conventional food, cloth vs. disposable diapers, sleep training, and co-sleeping—all issues that some parents feel pressured and guilty about but instead should decide prayerfully on these matters before the Lord. Be aware of the temptation in your own heart to compete with others also in these areas of parenting. This competition may be an obstacle to relational and spiritual flourishing of the family and even of the church community.

As the child grows and begins to display their personality and sin nature, in their own 'creative' ways, *be discerning* and *learn to recognize manipulation.* Be careful yourself, not to bribe them just to keep the peace. And be prepared to say 'no' when your child asks you to buy extra items in the grocery store checkout line and craves yet another item after you've just bought several.[27] Be consistent in keeping determined boundaries. Feel free to let your child see your dependence on the Lord as you seek Him in parenting. You may even turn to God in spontaneous prayer at times when you need guidance, even out loud in the very presence of your infant, toddler, or older child. Remember: You'll help them not to become a self-centered, materialistic, always-want-more individual by these kind of attitudes and boundaries. Model servanthood and sacrifice to them in your personal life and remind them verbally that their happiness doesn't depend on getting everything they want.

Talking to your child about their innate proclivity toward selfishness and sin may be the initial step that helps them realize that they need a Savior. If they've trusted Christ already, such spiritual instruction, discussion, and guidance will help them learn to confess their sin and turn to Him for help as a way of life. Tell them and show them that you, too, are weak and vulnerable without Christ and that we all

---

27 Paul Tripp, *Parenting*, speaks of 'establishing authority early in little things' (p. 118) and of exercising authority consistently (p. 120).

depend on Him to be delivered from ourselves so we can truly live for Him and for others.

Helping your child focus on others rather than themselves through sharing and giving an item such as a toy or a favorite treat is a good start. Encourage them to do something for their sibling, even, or especially, if it involves sacrifice. When the opportunity arises, bring them along in your service at church, Bible studies, prayer meetings, and on service projects or mission trips. The younger child can be encouraged to serve in small yet helpful ways such as setting up chairs for a meeting or preparing food with you for a ministry group. As you do, articulate your reason for helping others and help them experience the joy of giving and serving people. As *you* serve the Lord from the heart, *they* can experience the overflow of your joy and fulfillment that inevitably comes. They can begin to experience the internal satisfaction for themselves in smaller and gradually greater ways as they grow spiritually and experientially serving God.

The Bottom Line

Your child is a sinner. Don't fight this notion in your parenting—accept it and address the root problem, not merely the symptoms. How can you do this? Good question. First, realize that there are forces greater than your child's will at work. Apart from conversion and spiritual regeneration, your child can't consistently obey you, and even *with* conversion there's a need for continual guidance. A parenting approach that focuses merely on external behavior regulation and modification will prove inadequate. We begin by stirring our child's awareness that he or she is a sinner who needs a Savior, the Lord Jesus Christ.

Only true, heartfelt repentance and trust in Christ will enable your child to receive the Holy Spirit who will take up residence in him or her. In the Spirit's power, your child will be able not merely to conform to your expectations externally but to render genuine obedience. This, incidentally, is the same kind of relationship God desires to have with all His children, including you and me. In this way, as we've seen in the previous chapter, the fatherhood of God serves as the model, the anchor, the paradigm of parenting that is grounded in the reality of life in this world, which regrettably but unalterably includes the reality of brokenness and sin.

What's Next?

1. What, if any, adjustments do you need to make in your view of your children after reading this chapter? Have you been too optimistic, too pessimistic, or accurate about their innate proclivity toward sin?

2. How does the realization of your child's thoroughgoing sinfulness affect your understanding of your role as parent? Do you need to adjust your expectations or your approach toward your children in any way, and if so, how?

3. What can you do to implement parenting discipline techniques as described in this chapter with the goal of changing hearts rather than simply enforcing outward conformity through punishment?

3

I'm Overwhelmed!

Parenting in an imperfect world

What's Up?

Parenting takes place in an imperfect world, within a web of ungodly values, alongside indwelling sin, and in the presence of potential attacks by the devil. As you begin this chapter, reflect on the following passages to come to terms with these realities in parenting.

1. Read 1 John 2:15–17. How can this passage be applied to the challenge and opportunity of parenting children in the world in which we live? Give specific examples.
2. Read Proverbs 3:5–6. Reflect on this passage's relevance to your own life, then ask how this passage also relates to your role as a parent, and to your children's lives as well.

The Big Picture

'I'm overwhelmed!' All of us have felt that way, let's be real. Not only do we as parents need to be realistic about our own role in parenting and be realistic about our child's sin nature, we also need to be realistic about the imperfect world in which all parenting of necessity takes place. This isn't a perfect world—not even close—though evidence of God's reality and presence abounds everywhere. So, if, as a mom or dad, you feel overwhelmed in the face of the challenge of raising a child that loves God and pursues His purpose for his or her life, realize that part of the reason why parenting can be challenging in this world is because the world itself, as mentioned, isn't always a friendly, conducive place for parenting.

In fact, contrary to unrealistic, idealistic notions of parenting, raising children takes place in the context of real life, continual stress, and this imperfect world. It took us a while to realize this, but often the problem—if there is a problem—is not lack of parenting skills, or even lack of spiritual maturity (or a myriad of other options), but somewhat trivial factors at the intersection of fallenness and finitude, like stress, busyness, or fatigue. To cope with the pressures of life and parenting, parents need regular rest and refreshment. They need encouragement in relationships, instruction and mentoring, prayer, and community support. They will also benefit from practicing fiscal responsibility, dealing with their finances with care and integrity. Learning to make sensible, daily, lifestyle choices is also important in the messy and sometimes mundane life we live. Moreover, parents have a need to be sexually fulfilled, a vital reality of wholesome living in this physical and material world. So, before we move into the relational dimension of parenting, let's take some time to address all these imperative issues.[1]

---

1   The need for realism is also emphasized by Chapman, *Things I Wish I'd Known*, who lists the following twelve things he wishes he'd known about parenting: (1) that having children radically changes your schedule; (2) that children are expensive; (3) that no two children

The World, the Flesh, and the Devil

The Bible teaches that there are three major enemies that will be continually confronting anyone who wants to serve God and live for Him. These are the *world*, the *flesh*, and the *devil*. To make matters worse, these enemies aren't unrelated but rather closely interconnected.[2] At the Fall of humanity, the devil tempted the woman, and she succumbed to the temptation, and thus, the devil's reasoning and rebellion entered the woman's nature and the man's as well. Now human culture—the world system and its values and desires—has a self-centered, God-resistant bent, and the devil is the 'Ruler of this world.'[3]

> *'Human culture—the world system and its values and desires—has a self-centered, God-resistant bent, and the devil is the "Ruler of this world."'*

Parenting and Culture: Assimilation, Accommodation, or Transformation?

The relationship between Christians and culture is a tricky one. On the one hand are those who demonize culture, claiming that culture itself is demonic. If so, believers must have

---

are alike; (4) that potty training is no laughing matter; (5) that children need boundaries; (6) that children's emotional health is as important as physical health; (7) that children are greatly influenced by our model; (8) that sometimes parents need to apologize; (9) that social skills are as important as academic skills; (10) that parents are responsible for their education; (11) that marriages do not thrive on autopilot; and (12) that children can bring great joy. We certainly say a hearty 'Amen!' to the last affirmation. We'll touch on many of the other observations in the following pages.

2   Though see Tripp, *Parenting*, 123, who says that innate foolishness is more dangerous than external temptation.

3   John 12:31; 14:30; see also 1 John 5:19: 'We know that we are children of God, and that the whole world is under the control of the evil one' (NIV).

nothing to do with it and be always separate. Others say—or at least act like they believe—that culture is essentially good, or at least neutral, so that Christians can freely participate in the culture. Then there are many positions between these two poles that to varying degrees advocate a discerning, cautious participation in the culture, so that Christians can maintain witness without compromise. The biblical call is for spiritual—but not physical—separation from the fallen world system. As Jesus put it, believers are in the world but 'not of the world.' Paul asserted that 'our citizenship is in heaven,' and Peter called us 'resident aliens.'[4]

It's of course helpful to realize that the world marches to a different drum than that of Christ. Its goals, priorities, and values today are much different from those Jesus exhibited during His time on earth. The apostle Paul makes this clear when he writes,

> I appeal to you therefore, brothers, by the mercies of God, to present your bodies as a living sacrifice, holy and acceptable to God, which is your spiritual worship. Do not be conformed to this world, but be transformed by the renewal of your mind, that by testing you may discern what is the will of God, what is good and acceptable and perfect.[5]

What God desires from us is not *assimilation* or *accommodation* to the culture but *transformation*. As Christians, we should seek to be transformed rather than conform to the thinking of this world. This involves a renewal of our minds. We ought to think differently, and then we should act differently, because we're driven by different beliefs about life in this world. Life is not about self; it's about loving and serving God and

---

4   Jesus's words encapsulate the essence of His prayer for believers in John 17. Paul's words are found in Philippians 3:20; Peter's in 1 Peter 2:11 (see 1:1).

5   Romans 12:1–2.

others. When Jesus was asked about God's expectations for His people, He responded in this way:

> You shall love the Lord your God with all your heart and with all your soul and with all your mind. This is the great and first commandment. And a second is like it: You shall love your neighbor as yourself.[6]

Do you and I always love God with all our heart, soul, and mind? Of course not. But this is what we should do, and this is what God expects. As believers, of course, we have the indwelling Holy Spirit to help us live in this thoroughly supernatural way. Jesus said many other amazing things about the way citizens of His kingdom should live. Many of these are found in the Sermon on the Mount. We should love rather than hate our enemies; we should pray that God's kingdom—not ours—be advanced on this earth; we should act toward others as we would want them to act toward us; we shouldn't worry about earthly concerns or possessions because God will supply all our needs; and so on.[7] This is the new ethic for the citizens of the kingdom. Would you agree that this ethic is radically different from the values, desires, and priorities of the culture in which we live?

And yet, God so loved the world that He gave His one and only Son to die for us on the Cross.[8] This doesn't mean that He indulged in sin, of course, or that He acceded to the world's values out of peer pressure or a desire to be popular. Not at all. God was willing, in Jesus Christ, to enter this world which rejected, hated, and persecuted Him and to act redemptively toward sinful humanity. No doubt about it,

---

6   Matthew 22:37–39.

7   The Sermon on the Mount is found in Matthew 5–7. See esp. 5:48; 6:9–11, 33–34.

8   John 3:16.

Jesus told His followers, the world will hate you; it will hate you because you're not one of them and because you won't go along with its pressure to conform to its values.[9] You must be willing to suffer with me and, if necessary, even die for your faith.

In one sense, then, we *should* love the world. Like Jesus, we should be set apart for God's service and then live in this world so people can see that we're different because of His work in our lives.[10]

One thing we've found instructive as we've studied the life of Jesus in the Gospels over the years is our Lord's example. Jesus was no monk, recluse, or hermit. He didn't withdraw from the world and live in a monastery and devote Himself to prayer and fasting all His days. To be sure, He withdrew occasionally so He could spend extended times in prayer and prepare to go back into the world that hated and yet needed Him so desperately. In fact, Jesus was so compassionate and merciful that people gave Him the epithet 'friend of … sinners.'[11] The Pharisees who stuck that label on Him didn't mean it as a compliment, mind you, but as a pejorative term. They, the 'Separate Ones,' practiced their righteousness ostentatiously, priding themselves on treating 'sinners' with contempt—but not Jesus.

Raising Culturally Astute Christian Children

What kind of Christian are you? And what kind of Christians do you intend to raise in your children? That's a huge challenge, but it's a matter you'll want to think through carefully and discuss together as a couple. Most importantly, the decision starts with you, long before you teach your children (more

---

9   John 15:18–20; 16:1–2.
10   John 17:17–19.
11   E.g., Matthew 11:19.

on this later in the book). If you're dealing with this issue for the first time when you discover your son is addicted to pornography or your teenage daughter is pregnant, you've probably been too busy to give this important matter the attention it deserves.

We believe that we should be thoughtful and theologically grounded in thinking about our God-intended relationship with the world and the culture around us rather than merely making *ad hoc* decisions based on the circumstances or people involved. Two people can watch a given movie for very different reasons. One may watch it for self-gratification while another may do so to establish common ground with their friends so they can be salt and light and talk to them about their faith in gracious conversation. The same thing may be true if you choose to go to a bar or engage in any number of activities.

At the Fall, the narrative tells us the following about the reasoning process that led the woman to disobey God's command:

> So when the woman saw that the tree was good for food, and that it was a delight to the eyes, and that the tree was to be desired to make one wise, she took of its fruit and ate....[12]

So, we see that the woman rationalized living for self rather than for God by reasoning that the fruit she contemplated eating was delicious—it appealed to her senses—that it was attractive and appealing to look at, and that it would advance her knowledge. People have reasoned in a comparable manner ever since. The apostle John may have had this story in mind when he wrote,

---

12 Genesis 3:6.

Do not love the world or the things in the world. If anyone loves the world, the love of the Father is not in him. For all that is in the world—the desires of the flesh and the desires of the eyes and pride of life—is not from the Father but is from the world. And the world is passing away along with its desires, but whoever does the will of God abides forever.[13]

We started out this chapter by thinking about the three major enemies with which we must contend while living on this earth: the world, the flesh, and the devil. The devil will tap into the values of this fallen world to appeal to your flesh and to that of your son and daughter. Unless they're grounded in biblical truth, this can be a deadly combination. We'll return to the topic of spiritual warfare later in the book; for now, let's make a mental note and realize that Christian parenting in this world is deeply countercultural and involves taking a stance that is rooted firmly in God's Word rather than being grounded in our culture and the world around us.

Busyness, Fatigue, and the Need for Rest

Unlike our discussion about the world, the flesh, and the devil, other issues are less clear cut. This is an imperfect world, and we're human. That means, among other things, that we're limited and finite—we get tired and our capacity to handle stress is not boundless.[14] When it comes to parenting, this

---

13 1 John 2:15–17.

14 Note that the standard Holmes-Rahe Life Stress Inventory includes several items relating to marriage and family (stress points in parentheses): 1. death of a spouse (100), 2. Divorce (73), 3. marital separation (65), 7. Marriage (50), 9. marital reconciliation (45), 12. Pregnancy (40), 13. sexual difficulties (39), 14. gaining a new family member (birth, adoption, adult child moving back in; 39), 23. son or daughter leaving home (marriage, college; 29), 24. in-law troubles (29), 26. spouse beginning or ceasing work outside the home (26); any total over 150 points per year means you're considerably more liable to a major health breakdown in the next two years. The original

means that we can take only so much before we become cranky or lose our temper, or merely lack energy. A wise parent, therefore, will recognize their limitations and plan times for refreshment and relaxation to recharge batteries and to reconnect with God and with their spouse at a deeper level.

When I first started out on my marriage and parenting journey, I read James Dobson's *What Wives Wish Husbands Knew about Women.*[15] One thing I still remember about reading this book many years ago, is Dr. Dobson pointing out that the number one challenge with which wives struggle in their marriage and in parenting is *fatigue.* I remember thinking: What—fatigue, the biggest problem in marriage? That's certainly not what I expected to hear. I'm sure many other men felt the same. But when I went to my wife and asked her what she thought, she heartily agreed.

> *'A wise parent will recognize their limitations and plan times for refreshment and relaxation to recharge their batteries and to reconnect with God and their spouse at a deeper level.'*

So, husbands, if you're on the front end of the journey, please realize that you've got to have a plan for when your wife feels overwhelmed or tired. Come alongside her to help her, order Chinese takeout for dinner, get a babysitter and take her out on a date, or if possible take a day off during

---

publication is Thomas Holmes and Richard Rahe, 'Holmes-Rahe Social Readjustment Rating Scale,' *Journal of Psychosomatic Research* 2 (1967).

15 James Dobson, founder of Focus on the Family and Family Talk, wrote an entire library of books on parenting, including *Dare to Discipline* (1970), *Bringing Up Boys* (2001), and *Bringing Up Girls* (2010; all three of these published by Tyndale House Publishers). See www.dobsonlibrary.com

the week and give her a break. Ever since we got married, I've tried to give my wife at least one or two half-days a week—admittedly with mixed success—where she can read the Bible leisurely, go to a tea room with a friend, or get away from the incessant demands of household chores and beloved yet taxing children.

In the busyness of our days, it's easy to find ourselves operating in maintenance mode. Every day we get up, get ready for the day, eat breakfast, and then go to work, or start school or take our children to school, and throughout the day do the things that call for our attention. The next day, we do the same, and so weeks, and months, and even years, go by. Gradually couples begin to accumulate stuff. Eventually they run out of space. Some

> *'A full schedule doesn't necessarily mean that we're in the center of God's will or doing the things God wants us to do.'*

begin to fill a storage unit or may move to a bigger house. We've learned that, in view of this tendency, it's helpful to keep things simple, embracing a type of 'holy minimalism,'[16] regularly cleaning house and sharing the wealth of gathered things—or getting rid of them.

There are certainly more important things in life than to advance one's career and to chase the things that our flesh craves for gratification, comfort, expediency, and even self-aggrandizement. Have you made the decision to put God and your family first in this regard? If so, you've laid the foundation for setting a powerful example for your children, and more likely than not, they'll do the same. An undue focus on things can seriously distract us from a fruitful life of service

---

16 See, e.g., Randy Frazee, *Making Room for Life: Trading Chaotic Lifestyles for Connected Relationships* (Grand Rapids: Zondervan, 2003).

to God and effective parenting, but just as counterproductive may be a life of hyperactive, frenetic busyness (as much as some of us might think that this enables us to do more for God or for His kingdom sometimes).

As C. J. Mahaney reminds us, busyness doesn't mean we're diligent, faithful, or fruitful.[17] A full schedule doesn't necessarily mean that we're in the center of God's will or accomplishing the things God wants us to do. Doing everything people ask us to do, everything we want to do, and most everything that comes our way and isn't sinful or immoral demonstrates a need for screening devices in our lives, called 'wisdom' and 'discernment.' Examining all the opportunities presented and filtering them through the lens of what we understand God's calling on our lives to be is crucial for a life lived to the glory of God.

We've lived in the same house for the last twenty years, and my husband has held the same job for the same amount of time. I've spent most of my time nurturing our four children together with my husband, and serving women in the local church. Not everyone can have as much job security as the Lord has given us, but at least in our case, being content with what we have has provided a stable environment for our children. This has given them the opportunity to be schooled, grow and develop, and now go to college, being anchored and grounded in a family and a locale that is home. In this age of transience and fast-paced technological development, we're thankful that the Lord led us to this place of permanence that is an increasingly scarce commodity.

The reality is, this is where people live. We're doing too much, and often have too little time for the most important responsibility: our children. As parents, we can easily get

17 C. J. Mahaney, 'Biblical Productivity,' originally posted at www. sovereigngraceministries.org/blog

overcommitted if we're not careful. Our children, too, can get so busy with various activities—all good and unobjectionable in and of themselves—that there remains little time for reflection, rest, and quality time. Most importantly, their time with the Lord can easily get squeezed out or even vanish into non-existence. Nothing is worth such a hectic lifestyle. A busy life may flatter our egos, and serve as a sort of escape mechanism—no need to come to terms with our loneliness, unanswered questions, uncertainty regarding our calling, our future spouse, and so forth—but it hardly ever permanently and successfully serves as a substitute for doing a few things well.[18] Be still and know your God, and listen to Him.[19] Take time out amid the relentless clamor of life. Stop and look around. And take notice of what God is doing in your life and in the lives of your children.

And resolve to do a few things well—your relationship with God, time with one another and with family, and serving God in your local church with an intelligent, meaningful, and strategic focus. Take some time at your earliest convenience and ask yourself the question: Am I doing too much? Am I able to do everything that I'm currently doing with excellence? Or am I in perennial rush and maintenance mode? If so, maybe

---

18 Apart from Andreas's book *Excellence: The Character of God and the Pursuit of Scholarly Virtue* (Wheaton: Crossway, 2010), you may want to browse through Randy Frazee's book *Making Room for Life*. Frazee challenges us to examine the plethora of surface relationships in our lives, to get in step with the rhythms of life (work, relationships, rest), and to declare war on our crowded schedules. In chapter 8, Frazee speaks of the 'seven deadly sins' against our children when we drag them away in the late afternoon and evening and on weekends to engage in adult-driven, highly structured, age-graded activities: (1) lost creativity; (2) lost leadership skills; (3) lost mentoring; (4) lost conflict management; (5) lost health; (6) lost finances; and (7) lost family meals.

19 Psalm 46:10.

it's time for you to divest yourself of certain responsibilities and to step aside for someone else to give himself fully to that task that you're able to do only half-heartedly. What's more, resolve to model a quality lifestyle in front of your children and to encourage them to screen opportunities that come their way. Our twenty-year-old son has adopted the motto that he wants to seize the best opportunities that arise for him. That said, he is committed to screening everything in view of his current priorities and his understanding of his life calling (which is still being refined).

Just recently, he sent me the following note he sent to his supervisors (shared here with his permission):

> Dear Ms. — and Mr. —:
>
> Hope you're both having a great week! After thinking a lot about being a student leader this past week along with talking to you both and some others, I've decided that it would be too much for me to continue serving as a student leader next year, while taking on a new position as AC [Area Coordinator, supervising several RAs], continuing to be a Hamilton Scholar, upping my hours to 18 credits, and being involved at my church. *I would rather do few things and do these excellently than try and do many things and stretch myself too thin.* While I'm planning on taking a year off, I'd love to possibly return the following year to be a student leader as my responsibilities will probably have lightened up by then. If possible, please let me know your thoughts. Thank you so much!
>
> Sincerely,

You can tell that it wasn't easy for our son to write that email, but he wrestled with it for quite some time and finally concluded stepping down from this responsibility was the right thing to do. A couple months later, he's very glad he did!

Finally, there's no substitute for the trusty old 'To Do' list to help us stay balanced and keep the task of parenting central in our lives which it should be. I always keep a list of things to do on my smart phone, and whenever anything new comes to mind, I put it on that list, including things I need to do with and for the family. If it's on that list, it'll get done! These indicate my priorities, though nothing is too small to be put on that list. I derive great satisfaction from deleting

> 'Let God screen your tasks and your daily life and ask Him when you face major decisions.'

items from that list and see it grow smaller. By putting even small items on that list, I keep my mind free from unnecessary clutter which allows me to focus on bigger priorities throughout the day and the week. The Bible says, 'Commit your work to the LORD, and your plans will be established.'[20] It also says, 'Commit your way to the LORD; trust in him, and he will act… Be still before the LORD and wait patiently for him.'[21] Let God screen your tasks and your daily life and ask Him when you face major decisions. Your life is an open book before Him. Cultivate the lost art of waiting for *Him*, and *He* will direct your paths.[22]

The Need for Encouragement, Support, and Mentoring

So, we've talked about the need for occasional times of rest and refreshment. By this we're not thinking merely of the yearly summer vacation (though that's important, too, and many lifelong memories are formed there). We're also

20 Proverbs 16:3.
21 Psalm 37:5, 7a.
22 Proverbs 3:5–6.

talking about more frequent and regular ways which enable us to cope with the considerable demands on our time and energy as parents. Living at a distance from our parents in Canada and Austria, we personally have not had family close by to support us through our years of parenting (though the children have certainly enjoyed seeing their grandparents occasionally on special trips). Instead, we've craved and benefited from other kinds of support, whether through our local church community or friends.

My wife will tell you that it's been hard not having more support, and, let's be honest, there's only so much a husband can do, even though a supportive husband is certainly something every wife and mother will desire very deeply. In any case, if you're a young couple, be grateful for family support (of course, we realize there can be challenges there, too, as in-laws may not always share the same values as we do; more on that later). Husbands, again, recognize your wife's need for a break and for tangible support and encouragement. The Bible tells us husbands to be considerate toward our wives as the 'weaker vessel' and to treat them as fellow heirs of grace.[23] Our wives depend on us and on our understanding and active undergirding.

One husband I've known seemed to be always connected and engaged with his wife throughout the day. When he and I were on our way to lunch, he would quickly call home and ask his wife how she was doing and offer a few words of encouragement and advice. This left a lasting impression on me as I can easily get immersed in work only to re-emerge at the end of the day, maybe leaving my wife to fend on her own all day long without any expression of care or tangible support. Our partnership as parents is vital. By 'partnership' we

---

23 1 Peter 3:7.

don't merely mean pure delegation where the husband passes on to his wife the responsibility of caring for the children during the day, and in some cases schooling them at home, while he remains largely disengaged and disconnected. No, partnership means we tackle the task of parenting *together*, as a *team*. Staying in close contact during the day and

> 'Partnership means we tackle the task of parenting together, *as a* team.'

empathizing with one another will go a *long* way to make the challenges that are sure to come more bearable and to help you emerge even stronger and victorious in the end.

I, Margaret, have a strong commitment to the importance of mentoring women. I love the passage in the book of Titus where older, more mature women are encouraged to teach young women to love their husbands and children, to manage their household well, and to cultivate godly Christian virtues and character traits as women.[24] It clearly indicates here that there is a need in the lives of young women for training in marriage and motherhood. As far as mothering goes, I was especially needy as a young wife and mother. For whatever reason, I wasn't aware early on that my infant had a need for routines in nursing and napping; it was not until my child fell asleep in my arms at regular intervals that I observed there was a natural pattern for feeding and rest. I pretty much learned how to take care of my infant by trial and error. As you can see, I craved role models and examples to show me how to be the kind of mother God wanted me to be.

Often, the more mature and older women around are too busy with their own grandchildren or with other tasks to reach out to young women in the church (especially those

---

24 Titus 2:3–5.

emerging from a non-Christian background like myself); there is a dearth of mature women making themselves available to mentor young women. If you're reading this and you are a mature Christian woman, let me encourage you to make room in your life for mentoring one or several young women in your church or in your circle. This is a vital ministry—to pass on what you've learned in years of marriage and parenting to the next generation (of course, make sure you do that for your own children and grandchildren first). This desire to pass on a legacy of faithfulness in parenting, in fact, is a major reason why we wrote this book.[25] As Director of Women's Programs and Mentoring at a church-based seminary in Cary, NC, I now enjoy training women students in all these ways, with hopes that ministry to women in the church will grow in quality and impact, and help undergird mothers, families, and the church overall.[26]

---

25 For other helpful resources for mentoring girls, see Nancy Leigh DeMoss and Dannah Gresh, *Lies Young Women Believe and the Truth That Sets Them Free* (Chicago: Moody, 2008); Mary Kassian, *Girls Gone Wise in a World Gone Wild* (Chicago: Moody, 2010); and Carolyn Mahaney and Nicole Mahaney Whitacre, *Girl Talk: Mother-Daughter Conversations on Biblical Womanhood* (Wheaton: Crossway, 2005). Helpful resources for mentoring boys are Kent Hughes, *Disciplines of a Godly Young Man* (Wheaton: Crossway, 2012; though I found this book not always as accessible as I had hoped when I tried to go through it with my son); C. J. Mahaney, ed., *Worldliness: Resisting the Seduction of a Fallen World* (Wheaton: Crossway, 2008); Dennis Rainey, *Stepping Up: A Call to Courageous Manhood* (Little Rock, AR: FamilyLife, 2011); and Köstenberger, *Excellence*. My son *loves* Justin Buchanan's *Guys and Lies: Nine Lies the Enemy Tells Young Men* (Raleigh, NC: Bay Press, 2011); he also enjoyed and benefited from Brent Crowe's *Chasing Elephants: Wrestling with the Gray Areas of Life* (Colorado Springs: NavPress, 2010).

26 Shepherds Theological Seminary offers an M.Div. in Women's Ministry and other degrees which include courses on mentoring women in the church based on Titus 2:3–5. For more information, see www.shepherds.edu

The Big Three: Sex, Money, and In-Laws

Perhaps the three areas that are the trickiest to navigate in marriage with palpable implications for parenting are sex, money, and in-laws. Young parents often seem to be ill-equipped to handle financial matters. Popular shows regularly convey the notion that married people don't have sex. In-laws are nearly always portrayed negatively. In a book of this nature, we cannot expect to deal with each of these vital areas in exhaustive detail. Two families merging together may create tension, friction, and a clash of conflicting values in these and other areas. Compromised sexual history and background may contribute to the stress and conflict a couple may experience, and it likely will take a while for each to learn how to relate to the other in this vital area. Regarding finances, each spouse may be accustomed to different standards of living and spending habits. Parenting—particularly, having a baby—amid these various kinds of adjustments and stressors will likely be rendered even more challenging. Fortunately, helpful resources on all these topics are readily available.[27] Nevertheless, let's talk for a minute about each of these potential sources of strain on marriage and family.

In-laws and Family Traditions

You may remember the old saying, 'Women: can't live with them, can't live without them.' Yes, marriage, and the merging

---

27 Regarding marriage, sex, and family, see esp. Köstenberger with Jones, *Marriage and the Family*, chaps. 1–4. Chapters 1 and 3 cover marriage and family in the Bible, while chaps. 2 and 4 address marriage and sex and reproduction and parenting (with contributions by Mark Liederbach on contraception and artificial reproductive technologies). In addition, we recommend the ministry and resources available through FamilyLife. Regarding finances, see Art Rainer, *The Money Challenge: 30 Days of Discovering God's Design for You and Your Money* (Nashville: B&H, 2017). See http://themoneychallengebook.com

of two different people itself is a challenge. This statement, applied to in-laws, though, works well too, as two different *families* merge. The Bible says that when a man gets married, he *leaves* his mother and father and is united to his wife.[28] Not only does this reflect God's arrangement, these are also very wise words. While both of you owe a lot to your families of origin, and love your parents deeply, it'll be vital to understand that you've started (or are about to start) a new family of your own. This is a new venture for you, no matter how good the role models might have been in your families, and you'll need some space to do so.

You'll need to talk at some length about forming your own family traditions or maybe adapting ones you grew up with— things as simple (or complicated) as belief in Santa Claus. (We chose to largely refrain from participating in activities related to Santa Claus, so much so that our oldest daughter at five years of age when she once saw a man dressed up as Santa Claus thought he was Noah.) What about Halloween? (We'll let you figure that one out for yourself.) More importantly, you'll need to decide how you want to raise your children, with the wise guidance of your parents, yet without their *undue* interference.

Shutting your parents out of your children's lives would be extreme. (After all, we're expecting to be in-laws ourselves one of these days!) To the contrary, you'll want to ask for input and advice quite a bit (remember, you don't have to take the advice if you disagree). As older parents, it'll be wise to allow our newlywed children, or those preparing for marriage, some space. What we've found is that if you do, your children will come to you more readily. In fact, we've spent quite a bit of time with our children in college talking

---

28 Genesis 2:24.

about relationships, career choices, important decisions, and many other issues, often at their request.

Stay connected, stay engaged, stay involved—but be respectful of the fact that your children are now old enough to make their own decisions, whether you approve or not. At the same time, until they're married, there is a sense in which girls continue to be under their father's protection and guidance, yet this should unfold in an environment of grace and selfless love, not compulsion or authoritarianism. And if you're reading this and just starting out as a spouse or parent, we'd strongly encourage you to solicit your parents' advice early and often—*before* you are way in over your head into debt or plunged into some relational or professional trouble.

Practicing Fiscal Responsibility

Moving on to the second of the 'Big Three,' then, we come to *money*. The Bible says to avoid the love of money[29]—i.e., greed—but money itself is something we all need so we can pay our bills and support our families. Speaking of paying bills, did you know that money—along with in-laws and sex—is one of the biggest sources of conflict in marriage? It seems there's never enough of it, which is why we should try to distinguish between needs and wants. Often what becomes a source of contention is an expensive hobby or habit, whether the husband's leisure pursuit or women's love of nice clothing (though, of course, as husbands we want our wives to look beautiful, and wives want their husbands to have some outlet and opportunity to relax). Make sure that you're accountable to each other in this regard, even if the problem is not a gambling habit or something more serious that may require professional help.

---

29   1 Timothy 6:10.

It'll often be one or the other who is more capable of doing the finances. In our house, I've always been the one who has taken charge of this area, in part because I have a doctorate in economics (no worries, you don't need an advanced degree to do a respectable job at this). In any case, as a couple we try to confer with each other in the case of bigger purchases, and even shopping patterns (such as where we normally go to buy groceries). Over time, those kinds of things add up to significant amounts.

We have a general budget of how much we can spend. To avoid one of us being blindsided by expenses incurred by the other, we've tried to give the other person a heads up if we make a purchase exceeding $100.00. We pay our share of federal and local taxes. We have a plan for saving—and now, spending—for our children's college education. We also have a car fund (we just helped our oldest son buy his first car) and a rainy-day fund. We have a retirement fund. In all of this, we trust God to provide for our needs and look to Him for wisdom and guidance. We also try to give to our local church as well as support various individuals and couples or families on the mission field, whether nationally or internationally.

When it comes to parenting, finances are important, too. On a general scale, it's our lifestyle choices—avoiding debt, being content with a smaller house, having only one car— that will set a baseline for our children as they move on to establish their own patterns of consumption. These will be our children's expectations that will need to be articulated and managed as they meet that special person with whom they explore marriage. Another crucial area is credit card bills and going into debt. We've always had just one credit card, and we've never had a problem with it. We believe that paying off that one card is a lot simpler than keeping track of multiple cards. Also, we've always paid off our credit card monthly. We've also tried to pay cash for everything as much as possible (even cars, though we did take out a small loan when we bought our family van and a mortgage when we purchased our house).

Teaching our children about the importance of saving and delayed gratification and cautioning them against incurring excessive debt is one of the more critical issues in parenting by which we can protect our children from sliding into financial bondage. Personally, we place a high value on our children's education (as we did on our own) as a strategic investment into their future.[30] For this reason we've allotted significant funds to paying for college and have told our children that we don't want finances to be a major factor when it comes to choosing a college (within reason).[31] In terms of delayed gratification and fiscal responsibility, we bought and loaned our second car to our children (which they shared, took to college, and passed down) rather than buying them a car of their own. This was helpful not only in saving money but also in setting an example of frugality.

While we're talking about money, teach your children honesty in financial matters. This is one of the principal areas where we should exercise integrity. We should pay what we owe. We should understand the concept of *stewardship*—that we're ultimately managing money for God and called to be a blessing to others. Help your children be grateful for the ways in which God provides for their needs and their family's needs, and help them see how you're trusting God to provide. Help them also learn how not to accumulate an unreasonable

---

30 For more on this topic, see chapter 8 below.

31 Of course, depending on their circumstances, financial situation, and degree of parental support, some students will need to take out loans because their jobs don't allow for them to pay completely out of pocket.

amount of college or other debt, and counsel them to a delayed and moderate use of credit cards.[32] Dave Ramsey suggests the following ways to go through college without student debt: (1) scholarships and student employment or other part-time work; (2) parents pursuing extra income; (3) taking a sinking-fund approach (i.e., setting aside income over time to fund a future purchase or expense or to repay a debt); (4) passing on unaffordable schools; and (5) taking advantage of Advanced Placement (AP) classes.[33] It'd be easy to add other creative ways of minimizing student loan debt, such as starting an Education IRA when children are still young, paying in-state rather than out-of-state tuition whenever possible, and, of course, living within one's means and being frugal regarding

---

32   Kate Shellnutt, 'Forgive Us Our Debts: How Christian College Grads Pay the Price,' http://www.christianitytoday.com/women/2017/june/forgive-us-our-student-loan-debt-christian-college.html, who cites a report that in the United States in 2017, 44 million people owe $1.3 trillion in student loans (Zack Friedman, 'Student Loan Debt in 2017: A $1.3 Trillion Crisis,' February 21, 2017, https://www.forbes.com/sites/zackfriedman/2017/02/21/student-loan-debt-statistics-2017/#1705ead85dab). The average student loan debt for graduates of the Class of 2016 was $37,172 (http://www.makelemonade.co/top-reads/refinance-student-loans-forgiveness). Richard Fry, 'Young Adults, Student Debt and Economic Well-Being,' May 14, 2014, http://www.pewsocialtrends.org/2014/05/14/young-adults-student-debt-and-economic-well-being, analyzes a Pew Research Center analysis of government data, noting that the median student debt load in 2014 stood at approximately $13,000, with significant negative implications for wealth accumulation, home ownership, and overall financial well-being (higher credit card debts, car loans, etc.). Ron Lieber, 'Does God Want You to Spend $300,000 for College?,' June 23, 2017, https://www.nytimes.com/2017/06/23/your-money/notre-dame-tuition-father-jenkins-golden-dome-.html?_r=0

33   Dave Ramsey, '5 Debt-Free Ways to Pay for College (and Still Save for Retirement),' https://www.daveramsey.com/blog/5-ways-parents-cash-flow-college

discretionary expenses on vacations, entertainment, eating out, etc.

Another set of ideas pertains to creative dates and leisure activities for parents and families. Rather than vegging out in front of the TV or watching Netflix, we've found there are many inexpensive fun outings we and our children enjoy. Our local art museum hosts outdoor movie nights once a week in the summer, which is a terrific way of watching a recent (and decent) film together, plus enjoying a picnic before the show gets underway. We also love going for hikes, bike rides, and now that the children are older, even museums hold their attention a lot longer than they used to. A little while ago, we added a basketball court and a fire pit adjacent to our house. These additions have given our children and family hours of safe and healthy activity, plus have made our house a much more attractive destination for visitors, including our children's friends and families we know. You get the picture— there are ways to have fun that are healthier and often less costly if we take the time to be thoughtful and strategic when it comes to family outings and leisure activities, whether for us as couples or with the entire family.

Sex and Parenting

We'll close this chapter with a few words about *sex*. We're not talking here about sex in marriage in general but marital sex in relation to parenting.[34] Lack of sexual fulfillment can cause a lot of frustration and become the source of significant conflict. Husbands, realize that faithfulness to your wife is a matter of your heart, not merely staying in the marriage while finding part of your sexual gratification elsewhere, whether in

---

34 On sex in marriage, see Köstenberger with Jones, *God, Marriage, and Family*, chapter 4.

other relationships or in virtual substitutes.[35] Wives, please realize that sex may be more important to your husbands than you realise, and to yourself possibly, too. Therefore try not to withhold sex as a means of manipulating your spouse.[36] Being fulfilled in your sexual relationship is a vital part of your union and unity as a couple and as parents. In this way, you can partner in complementing each other as mom and dad to your children. And don't be afraid to show occasional affection toward each other in front of your children. They'll be happy to see their parents have a good relationship and really love each other.

One more thing: Wives, don't be too preoccupied with your children when spending time with your husband. It may be easier for us men to compartmentalize between parenting and having sex, but as much as possible, once parenting issues have been dealt with for the time being, it'll be important for the wife to put the children aside to focus on being with her husband—that's part of setting appropriate boundaries. At the same time, husbands, realize that it'll be hard for your wife to be intimate with you if there are unresolved issues that she's still working through in her mind. Also, sometimes it'll be hard to find time for sex if the children are around 24/7 and don't go to bed until 10 o'clock at night or even later. You'll have to train your chil-

> *'Being fulfilled in your sexual relationship is a vital part of your union and unity as a couple and as parents.'*

dren to accept that there'll be times when the bedroom door is locked. That'll teach them that mom and dad have a relationship, too, and that they should respect your privacy.

---

35 See Jesus's teaching in Matthew 5:27–28.

36 See Paul's teaching in 1 Corinthians 7:3–5.

I once knew a man who worked as a real estate agent. He won many 'Agent of the Month' or even 'Agent of the Year' awards for his tireless efforts. But his success at work came with a price tag at home. When his phone rang, even if it was during lunch on Sunday after church, he would take the call and, if duty called, leave the meal to attend to some urgent business. For a while, I lost track of my friend, but when we reconnected years later, he told me that his wife had left him. She eventually got tired of always playing second fiddle to my friend's work and clients. That's a sobering tale.

The lesson to be learned is this: We must set proper priorities in our lives, and marriage and family must be a key priority. All of us want to think that we've got our priorities straight, but do we? Does your spouse feel he or she has your undivided attention—ever? Or are you habitually distracted or preoccupied with work responsibilities or worries about the children or aging parents or a litany of other concerns? Let's commit our cares to God, and set proper boundaries, and then cherish and celebrate the good gifts He's given us in our life partner and our family. As the wise Preacher wrote many years ago, 'Enjoy life with the wife whom you love, all the days of your vain life that he has given you under the sun.'[37]

The Bottom Line

Kiss perfect, idealistic parenting goodbye. Say hello to parenting in an imperfect world. Be realistic. Parenting is not just about parents and children; it's also about the imperfect world we live in. This world has many challenges that make parenting, with all our ideals, dreams, and expectations, a lot

> 'We must set proper priorities in our lives, and marriage and family must be a key priority.'

harder than it might otherwise be. First, there are the world,

---

37 Ecclesiastes 9:9.

the flesh, and the devil, steadfastly seeking to undo what we try to instill in our children, causing us and them to stumble and fall, and succumb to various kinds of temptation.

Then, because we're human and finite, there are natural limitations such as lack of energy, fatigue, and need of rest—limitations we need to recognize and anticipate if we don't want to be a cranky, frantic, maxed-out parent who is way too busy to realize that he has turned into a rather unpleasant person to live with and be around. Parents generally don't lack in good intentions; it's just that because of the stress and demands life throws at them they often aren't able to make good on those intentions as life gradually gets busier and busier.

This is also true regarding the 'Big Three'—sex, money, and in-laws. Again, a realistic approach to parenting will recognize that challenges will come in these areas and will try to be proactive and sensible in these pressure points of life.

What's Next?

1. What do you find to be the greatest successes and challenges in parenting? Are these internal obstacles (such as selfishness or fatigue) or external obstacles (such as financial pressures or spiritual warfare) or both? How do these challenges affect your parenting?

2. Make a list of the people on whom you can call to support you as parents, such as your parents or in-laws, friends, people at church, or others (including babysitters). Do you have sufficient help or do you need to strengthen your network of support?

3. Discuss any sources of frequent conflict, such as your relationship with your in-laws, financial matters, or your sexual relationship. What stresses are you facing? What can you do to improve? List specific steps and plan to implement them.

Part 2
Relational Parenting
Loving your children

Introduction to Part 2

God created us for community. We all need meaningful relationships and a social network of people who love us and care for us. The primary place where we can find love and acceptance is our family. No one knows us better than our children, and if you're a young man or young woman, the fact is that no one knows you better—and loves you more—than your parents (besides God, of course!). Yes, it's true! For this reason, it's so vital that we acknowledge that loving our children is a high priority in our approach to parenting. In one sense, to even say this seems redundant because virtually all parents love their children. But loving our children means not only *telling* them that we love them but *showing* that we do, and our actual practice may fall short of our best intentions.

The second major tension you'll encounter in parenting then, after that between realism and idealism, is finding the balance between *relationship* and *rules*. Many parents approach parenting primarily as a task to be accomplished.

They hope that if they follow certain steps, they will succeed. The problem is, children are a lot more complex than that! There's simply no magic formula, or series of steps, that by itself will guarantee success as a parent. In any case, how do you define success when it comes to parenting? In this portion of our book, we'll propose that parenting is essentially relational, and as parents we should put a priority on encouraging our children's relationship with God, cultivating our relationship with our children, and equipping them to deal effectively with conflict which is sure to come.

> 'More than anything, parenting is presence.'

Conceiving of parenting at its root as a relationship is especially important as our children grow older. The rules of the game change as they mature and can be more responsive to our rationale and reasoning. Many of us find that it's easier simply to keep everything under control by making sure our children are taken care of, rather than to *spend time* with them. Parenting is *very* time-consuming! If you plan to do parenting 'on the clock,' as it were, chances are your relationship with your children won't be as deep and legitimate as could be. More than anything then, parenting is *presence*. As one person once remarked, 'Ninety percent of life is just showing up.' Apply this to parenting. Are you going to show up and be counted as a parent? Or are you going to parent by remote control, by keeping your children happy or by giving them things whenever they demand?[1]

Chances are, you're in it for the long haul if you're reading this book. That's great! Our relationships with our children can be wonderfully rewarding if we pursue a *relationship* with them rather than keeping them at arm's length. What does

---

1   Like the bumper sticker my son and I once saw that said, 'My children think I'm an ATM.'

that look like? First, dads, it means that we will be careful not to compartmentalize. We need to care more for our family and less about our career. Women will have an easier time with this, as most seem to be already hardwired for relationship. In fact, most of what I know about being a relational parent I learned from my wife.

4
God-Centered Parenting
Fostering your child's relationship with God

What's Up?

It's so important for parents to take responsibility to introduce their children to Christ. Only when a child trusts Christ will they be able to glorify God and enjoy Him forever—living out their primary destiny. All their relationships with others, including parents, will spring from a transformed and renewed heart. And the Holy Spirit will become a powerful ally in spiritual transformation and begin to shape character. As you read the passages below, reflect on how God may be at work in your child's life.

1. Read 2 Peter 1:3–11. How do you balance grace and effort in the Christian life, and how do you encourage the same balance in the lives of your children?
2. Read 1 Timothy 4:12. How can you encourage your children to develop Christian virtues and grow in character and integrity even in their younger years?

The Big Picture

As important as it is to practice relational parenting and to develop a close relationship with your child, the horizontal relationships of *family* should never occur as the ultimate experience of parenting. The core of parenting should rather revolve around introducing your child to *God* in *Christ* and shepherding their growth in Christ (encouraging the vertical relationship of your child's relationship with his Creator). God has given you, the parent, a role to be used as His *instrument* in your child's life.

Toward that end, we can instruct, set the example, and inspire our children. The overflow of our own relationship with Christ will be evident as we live it out before them and pour our lives into them. A primary goal, then, is to be a part of leading our child toward a relationship with God; first by introducing them to their Savior. This involves teaching our child about their own innate sinfulness and the need for repentance and faith in Jesus Christ (more on this later).

That said, you can't put God in a box. If He so chooses, He'll open your child's mind to spiritual realities anytime, anywhere, whichever way He sees fit. One of our children received Christ while on a break during church (in the bathroom!). He was barely four years old, and he and I were in worship at church. He told me he needed to leave (for a restroom break), so I went with him. While there, he had my undivided attention and took the opportunity to ask me a spiritual question. One thing led to another, and by the time we left the bathroom, I had answered his questions and led him to a saving knowledge of Christ. Of course, the conversation didn't pop up in a vacuum (and the church service probably

> 'As a parent, this is what you want to see in your children: not merely external compliance, but inner transformation.'

stirred his thinking); but we had talked about the gospel before *and* there have been many spiritual conversations since that time. In any case, for the Christian parent there certainly is no greater joy than seeing your child come to Christ and then grow in Him.[1]

When your children trust in Christ for salvation, the Holy Spirit will enter their life and work from within to begin to transform them into ever-greater conformity to the character of Christ. It is key to understand that all our instructions are merely external to the child, and that without Christ they lack the inner capacity and power on their own to consistently obey them. But the Spirit can do His work within them upon salvation. He can convict them of their sin and give them both the desire and the ability to do what's right. As Paul writes in one of his letters,

> work out your own salvation with fear and trembling, for it is God who works in you, both to will and to work for his good pleasure.[2]

As a parent, this is what we want to see in our children: not merely external compliance, but inner transformation.[3] In this regard, the Spirit is our all-important source and ally. The Old Testament prophet Jeremiah envisioned the new covenant which would inaugurate the 'age of the Spirit' characterized by such inner transformation:

> For this is the covenant that I will make with the house of Israel after those days, declares the LORD: I will put my law

---

1 The same is true in the spiritual realm: 3 John 4: 'I have no greater joy than to hear that my children are walking in the truth.'

2 Philippians 2:12–13.

3 As Paul Tripp helpfully reminds us, 'Change is a process and not an event' (*Parenting*, 85).

within them, and I will write it on their hearts. And I will be their God, and they shall be my people.[4]

What makes your child a Christian is *not* being born of Christian parents, growing up in a Christian family, or going to church. Until they repent of their sin and place their trust in the finished Cross-work of Christ for themselves, their heart remains unregenerate and their sinful nature holds them in bondage to act on the prompting of their sinful nature.

A Gospel Conversation

As you talk to your child, here is what you'll want to make sure you address[5]:

1. **Does he understand that he is a sinner?** Or does he think he occasionally does the wrong thing but is basically OK? If so, explain that the reason why he does wrong things is because he is a sinner. In that sense, he is *not* OK. Something is wrong with him deep (as with everyone) down inside; it's called his 'sinful nature.' Pray that God will give him a sense of his own sinfulness, which will prepare him to understand his need for salvation. In proper balance this is in effect a preparatory step for the gospel. Be sure to acknowledge you own sinful nature. It is not that your child is worse that anyone else.

2. **Does he understand what Jesus did for him on the Cross?** Or is he as I (Andreas) was growing up—totally mystified as to why Jesus was pictured hanging on a Cross (even though I grew up in a nominal Roman Catholic home)? Explain to him that God, in His love, sent His only

---

4   Jeremiah 31:33.

5   Another tool we've found to be helpful is the three circles diagram: http://lifeonmissionbook.com/conversation-guide, which moves from God's design to brokenness to the gospel. There is also an App.

Son, the Lord Jesus, to die for him on the Cross, as his sinless substitute, bearing the punishment he deserved, so he can be reconciled to God and live in relationship with Him the way God intends Him to. Stir in him a desire to know God intimately and directly; this can only happen if he repents and places his trust in Christ.

3. Does he understand what he needs to do to become a Christian? Or is he fuzzy about this? Does he think this is something his parents can do for him? Or does he think he simply needs to try harder to be good and stop doing wrong things? Explain to him the wonderful concept of God's grace, in which salvation is a gift that is totally undeserved and cannot be earned. Explain that we need salvation but that God knew we can never save ourselves, so He sent Jesus to save us. All he is expected to do is gratefully accept and receive God's gracious provision through repentance and faith. Praise God!

Of course, even if a person is converted, it's not the case that once the Spirit comes to live within them, they no longer sin. Far from it. They're spiritual infants whose relationship with the Lord must be gently and consistently nourished. As Peter writes,

> since you have been born again, not of perishable seed but of imperishable, through the living and abiding word of God…
> Like newborn infants, long for the pure spiritual milk, that by it you may grow up into salvation—if indeed you have tasted that the Lord is good.[6]

If your child is a genuine child of God, there'll be hunger for reading the Bible and praying, though their sinful nature and impulses will fight against this, just as in our own lives as

---

6   1 Peter 1:23; 2:2–3.

believers.[7] There may be times when your child may be less responsive to the Spirit and when there's spiritual dryness. There also may be times when we unfortunately shut them down by not allowing room for the expression of the Spirit in their lives. So, be intentional in encouraging them to read the Bible and letting the Word of God do its work in their hearts and minds. And pray! When they're old enough, you can get them a good Study Bible and show them how to consult the footnotes if they have a question about a passage in the text.[8] You can consider educating yourself biblically, so that you'll be able to engage their spiritual questions as they arise.[9] You never know when they may come. Also, model and encourage them to be real in prayer—moving beyond set, formulaic prayers—and to pray not only for themselves and their family but for the needs of others as well, using Scripture.

Over the years, we've had the privilege of hosting missionaries, pastors and their families, and other servants of the Lord in our home, including my husband's students, church staff members in the churches we served, as well as

---

7   See Dennis and Barbara Rainey, '5 Ways to Help Your Child Develop a Growing Relationship with Christ,' http://www.familylife.com/articles/topics/parenting/foundations/spiritual-development/5-ways-to-help-your-child-develop-a-growing-relationship-with-christ, who mention prayer, Bible study, church involvement, mission-mindedness, and conference attendance.

8   There are several excellent Study Bibles on the market, including the *ESV Study Bible*, the *NIV Study Bible*, and the *CSB Study Bible*.

9   For a start, www.biblicalfoundations.org features many free resources on an array of biblical topics such as apologetics (defending the faith), biblical interpretation, biblical theology, Christmas, Easter, Jesus, marriage and family, mission and discipleship, and topics of special interest for women. There are also many helpful courses offered at www.biblemesh.com and many Bible colleges and seminaries committed to the authority of Scripture and the lordship of Christ.

Christian friends who were going on short-term or longer mission assignments seeking support and encouragement. This has been a wonderful opportunity for our children to see how people have dedicated their lives to serve Him. They've seen up close that missionaries are people with needs and questions, just like the rest of us, and have been able to interact with them about the Lord's work. They've also seen us come alongside those servants of God with encouragement and occasionally even financial support.

Serving Together

One thing we've found to be particularly important for spiritual nurture and growth is serving together as a family. As I get occasional invitations to speak at local churches, whether in the US or other countries, I welcome one or several of my children to accompany me. Especially when my sons (and sometimes daughters) were younger, I would often take them with me on those trips. We'd spend several hours driving to the site together, often engaged in great conversation. Upon our arrival, we'd check into our hotel and later go to the church or venue to meet with my contact person there. One of the things my sons really enjoyed helping me with is setting up a book table. Not only would they put up the table, they would also man the booth before and after I spoke. They got to talk to some of the people who attended the meeting or conference, and often people would speak kindly to my boys and encourage them spiritually. In this way, my children felt they were a vital part of my ministry and saw first-hand what I do in serving the Lord. When my older son was a teenager, he also started helping me with my website (www.biblicalfoundations.org). In fact, he redesigned the site and developed and maintained it for quite a while. One of his favorite parts has been to help me with the book giveaways of new books I've written.

Rather than feeling like ministry pulled me away from them, I think that our children would probably tell you that knowing God and serving Him is interesting and even fun! We don't merely want to encourage our children to read the Bible and pray. We also want to encourage them to serve as an outflow of loving God in the local church and in mission and ministry, and ideally, we can do at least some of this together as a family.

We're thankful for Lauren, our oldest, who has always blazed the trail in our family asking intelligent questions about the faith. She is very discerning about people's authenticity and a strong advocate of accepting people the way they are. For a young woman, she has very strong family values and an admirable commitment to honoring her parents, especially her dad. She looks to build bridges rather than nitpicking non-essentials or trivial matters. She has a keen sense of social justice and is very principled and convictional. She is a very accomplished professional at her youthful age and has interviewed with and worked for several global leaders in her field of publicity and social media marketing. She is a faithful friend. She works hard and loves life and doing things she enjoys—going to museums, hanging out at the public library, having coffee—with the people closest to her.

We're thankful for Tahlia and her love for the Lord. God has made her very much a people person. Her delightful personality shines when she is enjoying interaction with her friends, especially in meaningful discussions solving spiritual questions and learning application of truth together. She loves to serve others by making meals for them, inviting them over for game nights, and supporting the girls in her Bible study by giving them rides to church. Tahlia encouraged the family to stay together spiritually by inviting us all to be part of her college church which we all attend, though not always at the same hour on Sunday.

David thrives on serving the young men in our church and especially doing the same at our local Christian camp (an oasis in the middle of the Raleigh suburbs). The boys love him back and are inspired to live up to his suggestions and ideas for growth in character as well as for knowing God better. He is also God's witness in college. His door is usually open, and many come to him for counsel or just to hang out and enjoy his friendship. God has His hand on David, and we're praying for a fruitful spiritual harvest through his life.

As my husband often says, Timothy is a force of nature. Quiet at first, but when you get to know him—Boom! His intelligent wit brings out the unique traits of people in a hilarious way that leaves us all in tears of laughter. He loves to help in the basketball ministry at the same local camp where his brother serves and to be with his basketball friends playing, holding each other accountable, and experiencing growth in manhood together. His interest in the Word of God has blossomed recently, and his detailed attention to its claims and teachings demand attention and provoke much discussion in the family. His questions are remarkably penetrating and insightful (Why did God make Satan? Did evil exist, even before the perfect world that God created, even before Adam and Eve sinned? What if Adam hadn't eaten the forbidden fruit Eve gave him?). His mercy toward those in need is lovely, especially toward his mother.

Discipling and Mentoring Our Children

Discipling and mentoring our children is a complex task. We believe that the Great Commission given by Jesus to make disciples starts at home. If we're not resolved to disciple our

own children, cross-
ing an ocean to go on
a mission trip or min-
istering to others at the

> *'We believe that the Great Commission given by Jesus to make disciples starts at home.'*

price of neglecting our own family is a travesty. That said, we can disciple and mentor our children only to the extent that they're receptive. In so doing, we've found that there is a certain gender-specific dimension that is crucial to observe. There are ways in which our daughters find it easier to confide in their mother, especially on topics more directly related to women: female issues, medical questions, modest clothing, inner beauty, and relationships, etc. The same kind of dynamic is at work with our sons and their father. We recognize, too, that the girls often desire the input and the shoulder of their father, and the boys love their mom and respect their mom's wisdom on life matters. This is just part of the complexity of children growing and various needs arising and changing over time.

When the boys reached a certain age—between twelve and fourteen—they tended to gravitate increasingly toward their dad and crave male companionship and mentoring. No disrespect toward their mother, but they needed man-to-man sharpening. This was not merely a matter of socializing or watching sporting events together, or of other recreational pursuits such as fishing or camping, but also involved dealing with matters emerging in adolescence such as temptation, confidence issues related to their performance in team or individual sports (striking out in a baseball game!), and general decision-making, scheduling, and career decisions, which becomes increasingly important in the upper high school and early college years.

Asking Questions

Of the two of us, Margaret is the more detail-oriented; I'm a bit more of a big-picture person. Whenever our children come home from some event, she excels at asking specific and caring questions about what happened:

'Where was it?'

'How many people were there?'

'Who did you sit next to?'

'What happened?'

'What did you talk about?'

'Were there any problems or challenges?'

My wife's penchant for asking detailed questions never ceases to amaze me. In this way, she can stay in close touch with our children and draw them out. At first, give them time as they may be reluctant to talk, but after a while they'll be fully engaged and typically start sharing freely.

As a matter of fact, one time when our son returned from a day at the Lamar Stringfield Music Summer Camp in our area, I, Margaret, was excited to hear how his day went, whom he sat with at lunch, how he enjoyed the orchestra and sectional rehearsals, who his stand-mates were for the orchestra and the chamber music class, etc., but it took a while to get there. He didn't want to talk *at all* and even fell asleep in the car on the way home. It wasn't until the end of the next day at camp that more of this information started to spill out in conversation. My desire was to encourage him and guide him, but patience was necessary to be able to interact on the level and at a time he was ready to do so.

Teachable Moments

When mentoring our children, we particularly enjoy using teachable moments. Not that there are always easy answers, and just being there is a huge part of the ministry to our children, but in short there are often clear directions we can give to them.

Did the referee make a bad call in your child's game? Life isn't always fair. We can argue the call (which will most likely be unsuccessful) or choose to move on and keep playing the game, and let your character and skills do the talking.

Did someone else get the position your child applied for? In the end, God is sovereign, and He'll do what He knows is best for us.

Did a friend disappoint them or turn against them? We know it hurts, but people will often disappoint you, so put your trust in God—the only One who'll never let you down.

Did you get a traffic ticket? Accept responsibility for your actions and pay up.[10]

Did you have a difficult day? With God, there are ultimately no bad days because He can use all things to accomplish His purposes, even if it feels bad.

Got a bad grade? Did you do your best? If so, keep at it. If not, you may need to be more diligent. And always, let's keep things in perspective.

Something broke? We can buy another plate or glass. Nobody died. Be careful not to exaggerate the problem.

You've got a problem, even a serious problem? We've got a

> 'You typically don't have to generate teachable moments—only recognize and seize upon those that life brings your way.'

lot to be grateful for. Be thankful your family has good health and in poor health trust God and do the next thing.

---

10 In North Carolina where we live, we have this wonderful legal provision called 'Prayer for Judgment.' You can plead for mercy with the judge when you've gotten a speeding ticket (if you haven't gotten one for the past three years) and, if granted, there are no insurance implications. That's a gracious provision we've come to appreciate.

Were you involved in an accident? No one got seriously hurt. If so, we're together in this and God is with us and for us—our ultimate hope and strength.

Over the course of a child's growing-up years, there are literally thousands of teachable moments, dozens every day, which wise, thoughtful, and committed parents can use to reinforce a biblical perspective and world view. You typically don't have to generate teachable moments—only recognize and seize upon those that life brings your way.

Practical Ideas

Intentionally equipping your son or daughter to grow spiritually may involve the study of a book or a specific topic in the Bible with them. You likely should go out or meet with them individually once or twice a week to discuss important spiritual and personal matters. Though much of what took place in our family in terms of making disciples of our children occurred in the natural context of living in relationship, there were times when setting formal goals was helpful. If you have the opportunity to facilitate a class or have a qualified parent help you in apologetics (defending the faith) or hermeneutics (how to study the Bible) for sons or daughters in small groups, this can be extremely valuable.[11] With careful planning, and facilitated conscientiously, these series of meetings were considered as legitimate for homeschool high school credit. In any case, these are golden opportunities to equip your child strategically for a lifetime of studying God's Word and sharing their faith.

During a period when the boys were younger and the girls were growing into young women, Andreas led a morning class following the Sunday service he called 'Kingdom Families' at church. Intentionally involving parents along

---

11   See the resources listed in chapter 8 below.

with their children both in terms of fellowship and teaching allowed the younger generation to learn from the insights of the more mature generation, but there was always mutual sharing as well. We enjoyed breakfast, prayer, and instruction together every Sunday. All four of our children were part of this, including times dedicated to prayer for those interested on Sunday evenings. We greatly valued this period of our lives where a time of worship and learning occurred together. The young women were also intentionally included overall with the older women of the church, for encouragement and mentoring; whenever there were service needs, fellowship, women's events, and retreats, the young women, middle school, and above were welcomed. This could also be done with men and their teenage sons.

Recently while at a conference where Andreas taught on God's design for men and women, much discussion centered on the acute need for resources for training and nurturing the younger women. We encouraged these mature women in the church to take the young women through a study of Titus 2:3–5 and told them about what Margaret has done in this regard at church. Margaret hopes to provide resources in this area and to post relevant material in the space devoted to women on our website (www.biblicalfoundations.org).[12]

The Bottom Line

Introduce your child to Christ. Pray actively for your child's salvation and look for opportunities to explain the gospel to him or her. Realize that if your child is not a believer, you'll need to rely on external moral instruction, discipline, in all love

---

12 She has also developed a women's mentoring course incorporating a women's discipleship curriculum at the seminary where she now serves part-time: Shepherds Theological Seminary in Cary, North Carolina. See their website, www.shepherds.edu

and kindness, as well as other ways of influencing your child, which is both fair and necessary. The expectations are still there because of God's holy and just character. If anything, this might drive a child to their knees to seek God's help, just like the law aimed to lead the people of Israel to Christ.

Once your child has trusted Christ and received the Holy Spirit, then the Spirit will do His work to convict, guide, and teach your child internally, transforming their thinking and their desires in a Godward direction. Not that this will solve all your problems as a parent, of course, but the Spirit will prove not only to be a powerful ally in the parenting task, but the power in which you and your children live out their lives for the Lord.

We know that is sometimes easier said than done, and in the end God's purposes are sovereign and inscrutable. God won't always conform to our expectations, and we also must leave the timing with Him. We may even do everything right and still reap an ungrateful and rebellious child in return. Esau may or may not have had amazing parenting but before he was born, already in the womb, it was known what kind of person he would be. At other times, we may make mistakes and yet God may be amazingly gracious and cover for our shortcomings. I know there were times when I was amazed

> 'Not that this will solve all your problems as a parent, but the Spirit will prove to be a powerful ally in the parenting task.'

how God continued to show kindness and grace to one of our children even though I felt they didn't deserve it!

Unfortunately, parenting can't be reduced to a formula: If you do A, B will happen. Human relationships are complex, especially in a world controlled by the 'ruler of this world,' which puts sinful people together in sinful families and communities in this imperfect world. And yet, if our child has a personal relationship with Christ, his eternal destiny is secure.

> The Lord is my light and my salvation;
>> whom shall I fear?
> The Lord is the stronghold of my life;
>> of whom shall I be afraid? [13]

If they're genuinely converted, and regenerated, they're God's own possession, and we can trust Him to guide and take care of them, with us parents as His instruments and guides along the way.

What's Next?

1. How would you assess the current spiritual state of each of your children? Do you believe they have trusted Christ? If not, what do you think is the reason why they have yet to trust Christ? If so, do your children live out their faith or have they yet to grasp the implications of their faith commitment?

2. What can you do to introduce your children to Christ or, if they are believers already, how can you encourage them in their relationship with Christ? Is there a book of the Bible or a good Christian resource you would like to go through with them on a specific topic?

3. Identify a couple of teachable moments you encountered with your children during the last week or two. How did you seize these moments to help them become more Christlike in the way they handled adversity or in some other way?

---

13 Psalm 27:1.

5

Up Close and Personal

Cultivating your relationship with your children

What's Up?

Presence is an essential quality in parenting. Parents have the privilege of cultivating a growing, trusting relationship with their children, exercising 'holy love.' The parenting relationship is lifelong, and though it changes over time it never ends. Read the following passages and reflect on how your presence in your child's life matters.

1. Read Deuteronomy 6:4–9. What does this passage tell us about God's conception of parenting?
2. Read John 15:12–15. Applied to parenting, what should be our primary focus in relating to our children per this passage?

The Big Picture

Parenting is certainly more than a defined task to be accomplished whereby parenting goals are clearly identified, achieved, and measured.[1] It is also larger than applying the

---

1 Vestiges of this kind of task orientation may possibly be found in

most effective method of discipline in order to produce a well-behaved child. Rather, parenting is in large part a growing, intimate, and trusting relationship with your child of supporting and equipping them for life. Since every child is unique, parents of multiple children need to be sensitive to encourage, and even discipline in different ways. One-size parenting rarely fits all! Since children (especially at a younger age) typically crave their parents' presence and it is evident that *many* lessons are caught rather than taught, we aim to spend much time with our children and be their friend

> 'Parenting in larger part is a growing, intimate, and trusting relationship with your child of supporting and equipping them for life.'

(not in a child-centered but a God-centered kind of way). Practicing a relational approach to parenting results in personal and spiritual rewards that are palpable, pleasing and powerful.

A Father's Presence

Recent reports highlight the scourge of fatherlessness in the United States and point out the serious implications for children's education and many other areas of life.[2] An astounding 24.7 million children don't live with their

---

Tripp, *Parenting*, 93–94, who calls on parents to adopt a 'project mentality.'

2   Claudio Sanchez, 'Poverty, Dropouts, Pregnancy, Suicide: What the Numbers Say About Fatherless Kids,' June 18, 2017, http://www.npr.org/sections/ed/2017/06/18/533062607/poverty-dropouts-pregnancy-suicide-what-the-numbers-say-about-fatherless-kids?utm_source=npr_newsletter&utm_medium=email&utm_content=20170628&utm_campaign=npr_email_a_friend&utm_term=storyshare (accessed June 28, 2017).

biological father.[3] The Department of Education states that 39 percent of students in grades 1 through 12 are fatherless.[4] In an interview, David Blankstein, a veteran educator and author of *Failure Is Not An Option*, states that children without a father are four times as likely to be poor and twice as likely to drop out of school. A recent study entitled 'The Vital Importance of Paternal Presence in Children's Lives' indicates that 7 out of 10 high school dropouts lack the presence of their father.[5] Girls without a father are twice as likely to be obese and four times as likely to get pregnant in their teens. In terms of racial demographics, fatherlessness is at 20 percent for Caucasians, 31 percent for Hispanics, and 57 percent for African-Americans.[6]

The situation in the UK is not much different.[7] According to the Relationships Foundation 'Cost of Family Failure Index,' family breakdown in 2016 cost £48 billion or £1,820 per taxpayer, exceeding the entire defense budget.[8] The

---

3   U. S. Census Bureau, 'America's Families and Living Arrangements: 2010,' July 1, 2012, https://www.census.gov/population/www/socdemo/hh-fam/cps2010.html

4   National Center for Education Statistics, 'Fathers' and Mothers' Involvement in Their Children's Schools by Family Type and Resident Status,' U.S. Department of Education, May 2001.

5   Edward Kruk, 'Father Absence, Father Deficit, Father Hunger: The Vital Importance of Paternal Presence in Children's Lives,' May 23, 2012, https://www.psychologytoday.com/blog/co-parenting-after-divorce/201205/father-absence-father-deficit-father-hunger

6   U. S. Census Bureau, 'America's Families and Living Arrangements: 2010,' July 1, 2012, https://www.census.gov/population/www/socdemo/hh-fam/cps2010.html

7   Matt O'Connor, 'The Shocking Cost of Fatherlessness in the UK,' *The London Economic*, September 9, 2016, http://www.thelondoneconomic.com/tle-pick/the-shocking-cost-of-fatherlessness-in-the-uk/09/09

8   Ibid.

Centre for Social Justice reports in a study entitled 'Fractured Families: Why Stability Matters,' that half of all children born in the UK are raised by only one parent, typically the mother.[9] Not only do a million British children grow up with 'no meaningful contact at all' with their fathers, there is a 'dearth' of male teachers in British schools. As a result, many children from fatherless homes struggle in school or drop out altogether, battle low self-esteem, have a tough time making friends, and are afflicted with anxiety or depression.

These data provide compelling statistical support for what is intuitively obvious and biblically indicated: A father's presence is vital for a child's flourishing, especially during the growing-up years and adolescence. There are not only tremendous social and economic costs but relational and spiritual ones as well.[10] We've already observed at the beginning of our book that the very notion of parenthood is grounded in God and who He is as our Creator and heavenly Father.[11] At this point in our discussion, let's further explore

---

9   'Skyrocketing levels of fatherlessness having "devastating" effects on children: UK report,' June 17, 2013, https://www.lifesitenews.com/news/skyrocketing-levels-of-fatherlessness-having-devastating-effects-on-children, citing The Centre for Social Justice, 'Forgotten Families? The vanishing agenda,' October 4, 2012, http://www.centreforsocialjustice.org.uk/library/forgotten-families-vanishing-agenda

10   For further data, see the website of the National Center for Fathering: www.fathers.com, esp. 'The Consequences of Fatherlessness,' http://www.fathers.com/statistics-and-research/the-consequences-of-fatherlessness and 'The Extent of Fatherlessness,' http://www.fathers.com/statistics-and-research/the-extent-of-fatherlessness

11   See the discussion of parenting being grounded in the fatherhood of God in chapter 1 above where we discuss the fact that as men and women, we're created in His image and likeness—like a child represents his parents' characteristics—and called to fill the earth with additional image-bearers (also our children) and to exercise dominion over it.

the notion of the fatherhood of God in terms of how God the Father and His presence with His people serves as a paradigm for the way in which *parents'* presence in children's lives is a key aspect of parenting.

The Bible is full of references to God's presence.[12] Living in God's presence is depicted as tantamount to being blessed, while being expelled from God's presence—as happened to Adam and Eve at the Fall (and as will happen to unbelievers at the end of time)—is being utterly undone. As church father Augustine of Hippo famously remarked, 'You have made us for yourself, O Lord, and our souls are restless until they find their rest in you.'[13] As a matter of fact, the Bible's entire story revolves around God's presence. The story is essentially about human beings created for the purpose of living in God's presence, then being expelled from God's presence, and in Christ being reconciled to God and finally, through the Spirit, being enabled to live in God's presence once again. Praise God.

You may wonder: Why are the authors talking about God's presence in a parenting book? The answer is: Parenting, too, is primarily about presence—the parents' presence with their children (and, of course, God's presence with *us* as we parent).[14] In some ways that should be intuitive, and

---

12 For a helpful survey, see Susan Maxwell Booth, *The Tabernacling Presence of God: Mission and Gospel Witness* (Eugene, OR: Wipf & Stock, 2015), chaps. 2–4.

13 *Confessions*, book 1, chapter 1.

14 See Tripp, *Parenting*, 188–192, who discusses the following parenting implications from the Great Commission in Matthew 28:18–20 related to Jesus's promise of God's abiding presence for those who follow Him: You won't be punished for your failure; you're welcomed by grace to new beginnings; you're not left to your limited resources; God gives you the precious and timely wisdom of His Word; you don't have to shoulder the burden of your children's well-

probably won't take too much convincing. If you're a parent, you'll *want* to spend a lot of time with your children because you genuinely enjoy being with them, for the most part. The problem is, you're busy, you've got to make a living, you have other passions you want to pursue, and you still have a marriage to cultivate while being a parent. So, for many of us, it's not so much a matter of desire as it's a matter of feasibility and the pressures of life crowding in that make the reality of parenting different from the ideal.

That's why we have confidence that 'parenting as presence' will make a substantial difference in your life experience as a parent. You see, it's easier to keep parenting at arm's length when the baby is small, especially for the dad (though there are also many dads who help a lot). You can have your cake— keep working hard at your job, go out on dates, play some golf—while your wife does most of the heavy lifting such as nursing the baby, changing the diapers, and making sure the little one is properly cared for in every way. And you can eat it, too—enjoy the romance of having a child with the one you love, take some endearing family pictures, and uphold the gratifying vision that yours is a happy, healthy family. As Homer Simpson stated regarding his—highly dysfunctional—family, 'As far as anyone knows, we're a happy, healthy family.' That's right—but he's not really fooling anyone.

It's easy for some fathers to excuse themselves from being present in the family by spending an inordinate amount of time on providing for the family. This mistake can be made even by strong believers who prioritize providing for their

---

being every morning; God will never turn a deaf ear to your cries for help; weakness is a blessing, not a curse; and success is determined by faithfulness rather than results. For an application to ministry to those who are hurting, see Dave Furman, *Being There: How to Love Those Who Are Hurting* (Wheaton: Crossway, 2016).

families, but because of a demanding career and church commitments, the children end up not seeing much of Dad. And he may be exhausted when they do finally get to spend time together. In a father's mind, he may think he is present *by* providing, and to some degree that is true, but the family may experience his absence profoundly, and see him providing *instead of* being present. This seems to be an unfortunate pattern in many families. While it is important for fathers to provide for their families, fathers need to take care to balance work with their children's need to be in his presence, and not just when he is exhausted from a long day of work.

I feel I've been somewhat slow on the uptake when it comes to parenting, and have had to grow into my role as a father, in part because of a lack of role models in my own life, and in part because of selfishness and unwillingness to let go of rival pursuits in my life. By the grace of God, however, I've gradually grown to realize that I need to let God and my children more into my heart and to allow God to give me a genuine, deep love and care for my family. This, in turn, has motivated me to make room in my life for them. We can always make room in our lives for the things we really want to do and are convinced we should be doing. So, especially if you're a dad or prospective dad, ask God to give you a genuine love for your family and for your children and to help you to make time for them—lots of it! And don't forget to pray for them.

My youngest son is fifteen years old right now, and there's nothing he loves to do more than be with me. Think of it! There's someone in the world whose number one desire is to be with me! Whether it's throwing a baseball in our front yard, executing various choreographed football plays, joining me on a bunch of errands, or going to the beach for a day or two, my son is genuinely enthusiastic about spending time with his dad. In fact, right now he's reading a draft copy of the very book you're holding in your hands while I'm working on the manuscript. Praise the Lord! That's the way it should be. Will I take the time—*make* the time—to be with him especially while he *wants* to be with me?

A Mother's Presence

In a culture saturated with feminism and egalitarianism, the value of a mother staying home with her children is typically undervalued.[15] The resulting neglect is especially poignant during the child's most formative years. This gaping hole has significant ramifications not only for the child's life, but also the mother's. A child left to the care of another person may possibly end up developing in a rather different direction and the mother will lack the intended fulfillment and blessing meant for her as well as the significant impact on the world she might otherwise have.[16]

We encourage you to *embrace the role God gave you. Don't be distracted by what the world says will you bring more satisfaction.*

---

15   Andreas J. Köstenberger, 'Feminism, Family, and the Bible: A Biblical Assessment of Feminism's Impact on American Families,' *Religion & Society Report* 23, no. 1 (January/February 2006), online at http://www.biblicalfoundations.org/wp-content/uploads/2012/01/34-Feminism-Family-and-the-Bible.pdf (accessed July 8, 2017). Please take a few minutes to read this piece. It is very eye-opening in helping us understand some of the cultural currents in our society that have impacted the institution of the family in our culture in incredibly profound ways. For a survey of the history of feminism, see 'The Three Waves: Women's History Survey,' in Köstenbergers, *God's Design for Man and Woman*, Appendix 1.

16   Exceptions to this are tragedies such as the death of a mother or extenuating circumstances that don't allow for this such as adoption. On adoption, see Russell Moore, *Adopted for Life: The Priority of Adoption for Christian Families and Churches* (updated and expanded ed.; Wheaton: Crossway, 2015).

Despite any efforts to rationalize the decision as a new mother to go right back to work, or to employ the services of nannies or day-care centers, even church-based ones, there's just no adequate justification in placing expediency, lifestyle, self-promotion, or other considerations above God's primary calling and His purpose for you as a mother.[17]

The Bible specifies the God-given design for the woman in the creation narrative, including her distinct and indispensable purpose.[18] This role as wife and mother resounds throughout the entire creation account, even in that of the Fall, where God's judgment of her consists in sanctions that reinforce her God-given roles—pain in *childbirth* and *relational* struggle in her *marriage* (i.e., a desire to control).[19]

The very name 'Eve' in Hebrew means '*mother* of all the living.'[20] The command given at the very beginning to '[b]e fruitful and multiply'[21] indicates that *procreation* is at the heart of God's purpose for man and woman in marriage. The *nurturing role* is implied as a role for the woman, as well as the creating of a *home* environment where her family can thrive.[22] Observe also the signposts of a woman's stature that point to her God-given function of nurturing children in her feminine reproductive build. If we respect the woman's

---

17 In some situations, families are left to cope with a single parent because the mother must work out of financial necessity (illness of spouse, death, military service, divorce, etc.). Often in such cases, children and families suffer, but it is still helpful to elevate the plan of God for family and strive by God's grace to make provision for needs that arise in such circumstances.

18 Genesis 1–2; see esp. Genesis 2:18, 20.

19 Genesis 3:16.

20 Genesis 3:20.

21 Genesis 1:28.

22 For a thorough discussion of the biblical theology of manhood and womanhood, see *God's Design for Man and Woman*.

biological function of giving birth
to children and her capacity to nurse
and care for an infant, we will make
room for her to be there for her child
in the way God created her. Let her
be a woman!

> 'There's simply no
> satisfactory substitute
> for a mother's
> presence with her
> children.'

When my second daughter was born, we were faced with
the prospect of moving back to Chicago after Andreas's first
ministry job in Canada teaching the Bible to college students. I had stayed home with our first child but now was
faced with the choice of either living on an inadequate salary
or contributing to our family income by working part-time
as a Registered Nurse. I thought that if I were to work even
just a few hours a week, that would be enough to supplement
our income without any compromise to the family. However,
I found that working even for a relatively small amount of
time per week not only broke my heart as I began to miss
some of the early moments of my baby's life (and my two-
year old's) but I also found myself rather stressed. I immediately quit and decided to trust God with whatever consequences would ensue. (Fortunately, they raised my husband's
salary soon after that.)

We know several seminary student families who, after
deciding to respond to a call to the ministry, had to cut
back on their lifestyle to come to seminary. They were
faced with similar challenges that we faced when Andreas
began teaching in a seminary setting. No longer supported
by a comfortable (or at least adequate) income, the couple
considered if the gifted and talented woman should go back
to work. It's deeply moving to see such a woman along with
her husband in this kind of situation decide to trust God and
live out the biblical design—to stay at home. We pray for
more of such committed individuals, not only for their own

benefit, for the children's sake, but for the church and God's mission overall.[23]

Jesus said, 'No one can serve two masters,' adding, 'You cannot serve God and money.'[24] Similarly, we'd argue that as a woman you can't be all God intended a mother to be and put your career first at the same time. Choices must be made, and these may involve personal sacrifices. Unfortunately, many don't realize that parenting requires this kind of sacrifice (or they are in denial in this regard), thinking they can enjoy the benefits of being a parent without counting the cost. Jesus also said that anyone who would build a tower better first count the cost;[25] the same is true for parenting. And yet, whatever sacrifice parents are called to make for their children is far outweighed in the long run by the joy and rewards yielded by their investment in their children.

So, let's not be short-sighted and put short-term interests above a long-term perspective on parenting. No childcare substitute can ever adequately replace the mother's presence with her children during their growing years. Those who abide by and joyfully embrace God's plan will be blessed, as will the children. Such families may stand out in a culture that often fails to acknowledge the wisdom, goodness, and beauty of God's design,[26]and in so doing, will testify to the

---

23 We include these examples here to inspire young couples but nonetheless don't want to burden those who must choose to make different, and difficult, decisions than outlined here due to unusual, temporary, or even extreme circumstances. We pray for each of you reading this book to make your decision before the Lord in light of the ideal, knowing that God is a gracious, loving, and powerful God who will sovereignly guide each one of you.

24 Matthew 6:24; Luke 16:13.

25 Luke 14:28.

26 Helpful resources in this area include Gloria Furman, *Glimpses of Grace: Treasuring the Gospel in Your Home* (Wheaton: Crossway,

God who designed the family, and will participate in His mission, glorifying God, and ultimately pointing them to their Creator.

Parents vs. Peers

Despite the vital importance of a father's and mother's presence with their children, we've observed that children, far too early in their young lives, are often removed from their parents' care and influence in various ways. Gradually, peers rival parents' influence, and eventually parents are relegated to the sidelines. In many cases, this happens all too soon and earlier than it should. Parents may still be cheerleaders, but the children are calling all the plays on the field. Yet not all the plays work, and often they would benefit from our experienced input and guidance. If your daughter meets a young man in college and she takes advice almost exclusively from her friends while expecting you merely to rubber-stamp the relationship, you might consider: How strong a relationship do I have with my—now adult—child?

It's certainly healthy for them to make their own decisions before God, and we should give them space to do so, though daughters, particularly, will benefit if they remain under the father's guidance and protection until they marry.[27] Adult children should learn to appreciate the wisdom God has given parents—particularly, but not exclusively, if they're walking with God. As the book of Proverbs tells us repeatedly, the wise person will seek guidance; in the multitude of counselors

---

2013); *Missional Motherhood: The Everyday Ministry of Motherhood in the Grand Plan of God* (Wheaton: Crossway, 2016); and *Treasuring Christ When Your Hands Are Full: Gospel Meditations for Busy Moms* (Wheaton: Crossway, 2014); as well as Sally Clarkson, *The Mission of Motherhood: Touching Your Child's Heart for Eternity* (Colorado Springs: Waterbrook, 2003).

27 See further chapter 9 below.

there is wisdom.[28] A modern-day sage recently pointed out to me that the difference between knowledge and wisdom is this: *Knowledge* is knowing that, technically speaking, a tomato is a fruit; *wisdom* is not putting it into your fruit salad.

Have you been able to instill discretion on key matters and genuine wisdom in your child? Wisdom in young people is an increasingly rare commodity (some may even say it's an oxymoron). At its core, Proverbs is written to instill wisdom into the 'simple' young person who needs instruction—especially young men—so they can get on a godly path for life and find a godly wife. In many ways, the purpose of parenting is integrally bound up with introducing your child to God (more on this in the next chapter) and with equipping your children to make good decisions so they can find and live out their mission and God-given purpose for their own lives (more about this toward the end of the book).

> 'In many ways, the purpose of parenting is bound up with introducing your child to God and with equipping your children to make good decisions so they can find and live out their mission and God-given purpose for their lives.'

When They're Adolescents

For me, one of the turning points in my life as a parent came when I read Paul Tripp's *Age of Opportunity* while on vacation in Florida. I remember reading this book and thinking to myself, '*Now* I see what my wife has been doing all along.' She hadn't read the book but was just naturally relationally oriented toward our children. In Tripp's book, the author talks about the importance of hanging out with our children while they're get-

---

28 E.g., Proverbs 11:14; 15:22; 24:6. See further the discussion in chapter 9 below.

ting to be comfortable with their identity during the teenage years.[29] He talks about parents staying up late into the night and spending hours talking to their teenage son or daughter—that's the love language they crave. OK, I admit, it doesn't come as natural for me as it does for my wife, but I've come to see that this is one important way we show our children that we care. We spend time with them and come alongside them and help them figure things out. Or, at least we're friends, confidantes, and sounding boards for their thinking and struggles.

In fact, I've since come to realize that I should anticipate extra demands on my time during the all-important teenage years in my children's lives and arrange my schedule accordingly. This means having more modest expectations regarding my workload and productivity where I have control (such as expecting to write fewer books or teach fewer classes for me). Certainly, we want to make sure we're there for special occasions such as recitals, games, graduations, moving them into their dorm room in college, and so forth. It may even mean deciding to school your children at home, which will give you many extra hours with them. Schooling at home has the added benefit of helping you stay close in touch with them regarding their intellectual and spiritual development. As a matter of fact, we have found that schooling our children at home is a very significant privilege in which we have been able to impact our children more deeply than otherwise could be possible. We have enjoyed directing their learning

---

29 In a later book, *Parenting*, Paul Tripp talks about parenting as one 'never-ending conversation' (p. 91). This realization can be very liberating because you can't cover everything in one conversation, and parenting involves a series of adjustments and incremental steps. In fact, as Tripp notes, parenting is largely done 'on the fly' rather than in grand big moments (p. 13).

with a mix of academic and real-life experiences, such as using family trips to historic sites to supplement what they learn in history or literature, and to travel and minister together all over the world. We'll have more to say about this later in the book.[30]

If you adopt a relational approach to parenting as we suggest, you may find that when your son or daughter goes off to college, your relationship can still be very close. In fact, it may even be closer than any time before, because, whether they say it or not, they often need extra support and encouragement during this exciting and challenging time. Your support can take various forms—wisdom and guidance in choosing a course of study or classes, studying with them for exams, going shopping with them, offering advice concerning relationships and career choices among other things.

Not that we're helicopter parents or anything! No, really, keep in mind who defines appropriate limits of your relationship with your child—beware college administrators attempting to sideline parental involvement, though some have legitimate roles to play—but it is the Lord God to whom we're all ultimately accountable. Let's keep God central in this picture always.

The book of Proverbs tells us that children and young people are simple, naïve, or foolish and desperately need continual instruction and guidance.[31] Many young people and college-age students represent the simple, naïve, or foolish person in Proverbs. Those who are responsive to wise instruction will gradually *grow* wise—especially if they surround themselves with wise and like-minded others—while those who are

---

30 See chapter 8 below.
31 See, e.g., Proverbs 1:4.

resistant will become increasingly foolish and suffer the consequences of their unwise choices.[32]

Being There for Them

Again, the fatherhood of God will be our foundational model in terms of providing, protecting, and shepherding as well as nurturing and caring for them. Just as God reassures His people, 'I will be with you,' so we can be there for our children. When Joshua was about to enter, and conquer, the Promised Land, God promised to be with him.[33] When Jesus prayed in the Garden of Gethsemane, He, too, was assured of God's presence.[34] In the book of Hebrews, we read:

> be content with what you have, for he has said, 'I will never leave you nor forsake you.' So we can confidently say, 'The Lord is my helper; I will not fear; what can man do to me?'[35]

Have more encouraging words ever been spoken? In the same way, we can assure our children that we'll always be with them, to the extent God gives us the opportunity. We can't always *literally* be with them, nor would they want us to. But we can be available and we can pray.

Parenting as presence doesn't necessarily mean that we'll always be by their side at every moment. The relationship obviously changes over time. As they mature, it may mean simply being there for them when they need us. We want our children to know that we'll always be there for them, no matter what, to the best of our ability, and according to God's provision. We're prepared to comfort them when they

---

32 Proverbs 13:20: 'Whoever walks with the wise becomes wise, but the companion of fools will suffer harm.' On parenting fools, see Tripp, *Parenting*, 132–136.

33 Joshua 1:9.

34 Cf. John 16:32.

35 Hebrews 13:5–6.

need comfort. We love to celebrate their successes with them and to help them learn from their failures. As grandparents, we'll gladly watch their children for them, giving them time for refreshment (I remember so desperately desiring this support as a young mom).

Also, one day we'll die. But we can *remain* with them even in the values and principles we have instilled in them, and through the character and wisdom we imparted: 'Train up a child in the way he should go; even when he is old he will not depart from it.'[36] In this way, we can be our children's best friend: 'A friend loves at all times, and a brother is born for adversity.'[37] This is true even when we must confront our children and speak the truth to them in love: 'Faithful are the wounds of a friend.'[38]

A Biblical Illustration

The essence of what we're trying to convey here can be illustrated by biblical and spiritual example, specifically that of Paul the apostle. Like a parent, Paul was always there for his spiritual children and mentees, cultivating a growing, trusting relationship with them. First, he mentored young men such as Timothy and Titus.[39] After this, he sent them out as his apostolic delegates. While they were geographically serving in a different location, Paul was committed to staying in touch. Whenever he could, he paid them a personal visit to see how things were going. When this was impossible, he would send a caring letter, with expressions of personal

---

36 Proverbs 22:6.

37 Proverbs 17:17.

38 Proverbs 27:6. See the caveat on p. 48, n. 28.

39 See, e.g., 2 Timothy 3:10–11: 'You, however, have followed my teaching, my conduct, my aim in life, my faith, my patience, my love, my steadfastness, my persecutions and sufferings …'

affection, words of encouragement, and helpful instructions. In this way, in keeping with ancient custom, Paul's letters became a substitute for his presence.

In fact, there were certain advantages to letter writing, because his recipients had his words available in writing and could read and reread them to keep Paul's words ever present with them. Take the following passage as an example: 'I hope to come to you soon, but I am writing these things to you so that, if I delay, you may know how one ought to behave in the household of God.'[40] In this way, Paul continued to be present in the lives and ministry of those who were his spiritual children and those whom he had mentored in the faith. In addition, Paul regularly prayed for these individuals.[41] The same principle applies to our natural children, especially those who, by God's grace, have been converted and now also are our brothers and sisters in Christ.

Thus, in truth, if you have children, parenting is a lifelong calling. We can never check off 'parenting' on our 'To Do' list. Mentoring never really ends. It continues way past our children's middle school and high school years into their adult lives, and in many cases even into the lives of our grandchildren. Even when we die, the impact we have had on our children during our lifetime continues in their lives and through them in the lives of their children, both natural and spiritual, and so forth. This is the beauty of God's plan for us as we reproduce in kind, after His image, and in His likeness, for His glory. How profoundly wise and attractive God's design is for us as parents who seek to live our lives in keeping with His creation purpose.

---

40 1 Timothy 3:14–15.

41 See, e.g., 2 Timothy 1:3: 'I thank God whom I serve ... as I remember you constantly in my prayers night and day.'

Holy Love

Virtually all parents have a natural love for their children. But what does it really mean to love your child? Is this something you need to learn? For some, love is expressed in giving and pampering children with privileges and experiences. Often, it seems, children are in fact calling the shots with their explicit or implicit expectations. But it is God's design that parents oversee their children with appropriate and healthy boundaries, for their own sake as well as the health of the whole family.[42] At times, you may *think* you're in control, but in fact you may be manipulated. If you want to keep the peace while shying away from conflict, your definition of 'love' is to do whatever it takes to keep your child happy. This mistaken kind of parenting raises pampered and demanding children who are used to getting their way and think the world revolves around them. When they eventually discover that this isn't the case, they'll be in for a rude awakening.

What does it mean for parents to love their children?[43] Too often we assume we know the answer to this question

---

42 See John Townsend, *Boundaries with Teens: When to Say Yes, How to Say No* (Grand Rapids: Zondervan, 2006), who describes the tension between parental desire for control and young people's craving of freedom and independence. He writes that young people 'need to learn that freedom is earned and that they can gain freedom by demonstrating responsibility' (p. 11). Parents can help their children 'learn responsibility and self-control so that they use freedom appropriately and live well in the real world' (ibid.). This is where setting firm and loving boundaries is essential, limits that constitute 'one's personal property line' (p. 12). See the classic treatment by Henry Cloud and John Townsend, *Boundaries: When to Say Yes, When to Say No, to Take Control of Your Life* (Grand Rapids: Zondervan, 1992).

43 See Bruce W. Davidson, 'Not from Ourselves: Holy Love in the Theology of Jonathan Edwards,' *Journal of the Evangelical Theological Society* 59 (2016): 571–584.

and fail to ponder the nature of true scriptural parental love. In modern parlance, the word

> *'True love for one's child is more than parental pride and emotional sentimentality.'*

'love' has been diluted and emptied of its full biblical meaning. In earlier generations, Christians spoke of 'holy love' to distinguish divine love from mundane loves. This holy kind of love—God's kind of love, prompted by love for God—was understood to be rooted in God's moral transcendence and, as the sign of sincere faith, was seen to stand in contrast to self-centered kinds of love.[44]

Such 'holy love' produces an exile mentality regarding the present world in which we live: This world is not our permanent home; we were ultimately made for life in another world. This holy kind of love is humble, showing reverence toward God rather than displaying a cavalier familiarity with Him. Holy love also leads to moral purity and engenders a hatred of evil. It is grounded in biblical truth rather than emotion and is fueled by reasonable faith. True love for one's child is more than parental pride and emotional sentimentality. Too often as parents, we have blended Christian and non-Christian concepts of love and created a syncretistic mess of what is meant to be a pure and holy enterprise.

The 'love chapter' in 1 Corinthians 13 is often quoted in wedding ceremonies to define love for a young married couple. But the chapter applies equally to parenting and every other relationship. Read the following excerpt with parental love in mind:

> Love is patient, love is kind. It does not envy, it does not
> boast, it is not proud. It does not dishonor others, it is not
> self-seeking, it is not easily angered, it keeps no record of

---

44 Ibid.

wrongs. Love does not delight in evil but rejoices with the truth. It always protects, always trusts, always hopes, always perseveres. Love never fails…. And now these three remain: faith, hope and love. But the greatest of these is love.[45]

The Bottom Line

Presence is the essence of parenting. If you think you can parent in maintenance mode, you're on borrowed time, and your lack of commitment to truly 'showing up' as a parent will catch up with you sooner or later. It may take some time before you pay a price, but eventually you will.

Be there for your child. Cultivate a growing, trusting relationship with him. Love him—biblically defined—and be his friend. There'll inevitably be rough and challenging times, but if you're fully engaged—which takes time, lots of it—you'll be able to help him make it through and teach him abiding lessons along the way. This, in turn, will build character (more on this in a later chapter) and equip your child to grow in his ability to make wise, well informed, and balanced decisions.

> *'Presence is the essence of parenting.'*

Be a relational parent: Can there be any other kind?

For us, we mentored our children as they were growing up, trying to instill in them our values and biblical principles, especially regarding living the Christian life and making wise decisions. We've found that even now that most of our children have moved or gone to college, there is a sense in which we can still be present with them. Wherever they will be in the future, we will continue to be 'present' with them through these abiding principles and values.

We can also be present with them through diverse types of contact long distance, whether skype, texting, phone calls,

---

45   1 Corinthians 13:4–8, 13, NIV.

or other means. In this way, we can continue our relationship with them, providing further mentoring and equipping.

Third, we are present with them through occasional visits. They may visit us, or we may visit them. These can be close times of reconnecting and of heart-to-heart sharing that are mutually beneficial and encouraging but continue the parent-child relationship, albeit now among grown individuals.

Finally, we remain 'present' with them as we uphold them in prayer.

What's Next?

1. Reflect on whether you have sufficient time to spend with your children. If not, what can you do to make time for them? What keeps you from being the dad or mom God wants you to be?

2. Discuss: Do you conceive of parenting as a relationship or as a task/job to be accomplished, or a combination of the two? Do you need to make any adjustments in the way you view your role as a parent and, if so, what course of action should you pursue?

3. What are some things you could do with your children? Spend some time brainstorming possible activities and make a list. Then, plan to follow through on your ideas. Consult your children as well; they will be glad to help you.

6

The Peace-making Parent

Dealing with adversity, conflict, and spiritual warfare

What's Up?

In parenting, conflict is inevitable, both between spouses and between parents and children. With God's help, families can resolve conflict through applying four key principles. As you read the following passages, reflect on the true source of all our conflicts and how families can deal with dissension by putting on the spiritual armor of God.

1. Read James 4:1–6. What is the cause of conflict in your family? How is real progress in handling conflict possible?
2. Read Ephesians 6:10–18. How does this passage on spiritual warfare apply to family life? In what ways does Satan attempt to wreak havoc and what should be our strategy?

The Big Picture

Per Wendy Best, law partner in a firm in Calgary, Alberta, 'Disagreement over child-rearing is a main reason couples get divorced. Issues and differences over parenting and money are the top two reasons.[1] If parenting and conflict are close twins, let's make every effort to address this need, more so in view of the value that our Lord placed on peacemaking when He said, 'Blessed are the peacemakers, for they shall be called sons of God' (Matt. 5:9). Let's turn our attention to peacemaking in the family.

When we started having children, we hammered out a joint philosophy of parenting over many hours of (at times passionate) discussion over every subject from ways of disciplining children, to choosing edifying movies, and a plethora of other issues. At the time, this seemed tedious, if not a distraction or even a waste of time. As we look back, however, God led us through a process of exchanging thoughts, dreams, and struggles with each other; so much so that we've grown closer together as a couple and have gradually become more and more united in our approach to guiding our children—God's precious gifts to us.

In this parenting guide, you've seen us advocate a realistic and relational approach. Both aspects of parenting—involving realistic expectations and a focus on the relational dimension—entail the realization that conflict is a constant reality, even in the life of committed Christian parents of children who are believers (and certainly unbelievers). Effective conflict resolution is vital, and a strategy of avoidance of conflict will prove fatal to the family. This reality requires peacemaking skills and knowledge, and a strong trust in the sovereignty and power of God. God makes no mistake, He knows the end from the beginning, and He is a forgiving and loving God. We need to learn to look at things from *His* perspective and seek to discern *His* purpose in our circumstances and conflicts. We also need to learn to deal with our sinful nature,

---

1 Dave McGinn, 'Brangelina's breakup: They're just like us,' *Globe & Mail*, September 23, 2016, Section L, p. 1.

be aware of spiritual realities and then engage in spiritual warfare. In all of this, we need to pray.

The Reality of Conflict

One of the most impressive features of the Bible is again its realism. There just isn't simply a rosy, artificial picture of what life on earth is like, but rather it tells it like it is. From the very beginning of human existence, we know that Satan introduced conflict and strife into our relationships with God and one another. When God first held the man, and then the woman, accountable for transgressing His command not to eat the forbidden fruit in the Garden, both failed to accept responsibility for their sin. Instead, they blamed somebody else. Take a quick look:

> *'God makes no mistake, He knows the end from the beginning, and He is a forgiving and loving God.'*

> [God said to the man:] 'Have you eaten of the tree of which I commanded you not to eat?' The man said, '*The woman* whom *you gave* to be with me, she gave me fruit of the tree, and I ate.' Then the LORD God said to the woman, 'What is this that you have done?' The woman said, '*The serpent* deceived me, and I ate.'[2]

Incredibly, in his response to God, the man manages not only to blame the *woman* for his sin but even *God Himself*: 'The woman whom *you* gave me' (emphasis added). Then, when the *woman* is held to account, she blames the *serpent* (i.e., Satan). This failure to accept responsibility for our actions has been part of human experience on this earth ever since.

---

2   Genesis 3:11–13.

Similarly, very early in human history, sibling rivalry was first recorded when Cain killed Abel, his brother.[3]

Excuses, Excuses

One of the most comical excuses for sin in the Bible I'm aware of is Aaron's response when he's confronted with Israel's disobedience in making an idol in the form of a golden calf in the wilderness. Here's the biblical account of what happened:

> When the people saw that Moses delayed to come down from the mountain, the people gathered themselves together to Aaron and said to him, 'Up, make us gods who shall go before us. As for this Moses, the man who brought us up out of the land of Egypt, we do not know what has become of him' ... So all the people took off the rings of gold that were in their ears and brought them to Aaron. And he received the gold from their hand and fashioned it with a graving tool and made a golden calf.
>
> And they said, 'These are your gods, O Israel, who brought you up out of the land of Egypt!'
>
> When Aaron saw this, he built an altar before it. And Aaron made a proclamation and said, 'Tomorrow shall be a feast to the LORD.'
>
> And they rose up early the next day and offered burnt offerings and brought peace offerings. And the people sat down to eat and drink and rose up to play.[4]

From this account, it's quite clear that Aaron was an integral part of fashioning a golden calf in Moses's absence. (Moses had gone away to receive the Law from the Lord at Mount Sinai.) When Moses, having been alerted by God, returns and sees what the people have done, he is furious and

---

3   Genesis 4.

4   Exodus 32:1–6.

confronts his brother.[5] Will Aaron own up to what he has done in leading the people of Israel into sin? Here's how he responds to Moses:

> Let not the anger of my lord burn hot. You know the people, that they are set on evil. For they said to me, 'Make us gods who shall go before us. As for this Moses, the man who brought us up out of the land of Egypt, we do not know what has become of him.' So I said to them, 'Let any who have gold take it off.' So they gave it to me, and I threw it into the fire, and out came this calf.[6]

Did you get that? First, Aaron blames the *people* who are 'set on evil' and who told him to make the golden calf. Who was in charge anyway—Aaron or the people? But it gets better (or, rather, worse). The way Aaron tells the story, the people gave him the raw materials, and he just tossed them into the fire, 'and out came this calf'! Though Aaron and Moses were at a more mature stage of life, I'm sure some of you who are parents have heard similar tall tales when confronting your children about something they did wrong. While it's hard to keep a straight face when these kinds of ridiculous excuses are dished out, they illustrate the problem with our sinful human nature: We have a tough time accepting responsibility for our own actions, and when confronted, we tend to put the blame on others.

Don't Be Surprised

Realistic parenting will expect conflict. We shouldn't be surprised when disagreements arise. Relational parenting requires that we pay proper attention to conflict and deal with it rather than sweeping it under the rug. In the family

---

5   Exodus 32:19–20.

6   Exodus 32:22–24.

in which you grew up, what was the normal mechanism for conflict resolution? In some families, conflict is simply ignored. Many seem to be afraid of any form of discord. Others erupt in anger, or even violence, only to later apologize and vow never to resort to anger or violence again. Sadly, while their intentions may be commendable, keeping this kind of unrealistic promise is virtually impossible. What should we do when conflict occurs?

Four principles for Conflict Resolution

You may want to consider the following four principles for conflict resolution we attempt to practice in our home.[7]

> 'Realistic parenting will expect conflict.'

1. **Analyze the issue**: Identifying the problem in the relationship is a vital step toward conflict resolution. This may take some time because the parties may not see eye to eye on what happened and where the responsibility for the conflict lies. Ask questions, then listen. As parents, we should try to mediate and ensure fairness while not taking sides in the conflict. Focusing on blame rather than restoration also can add insult to injury causing unnecessary and extended conflict. If your children genuinely perceive you as an honest broker who desires their best, rather than being negative, partial, or overbearing in the adjudication of wrongs, this will go a long way toward bringing the two parties together. Take the necessary time to cover the

---

7   I developed these principles independently from the five A's found in Corlette Sande, *The Young Peacemaker: Teaching Students to Respond to Conflict God's Way* (Wapwallopen, PA: Shepherds, 1997), 102–107: (1) Admit what you did wrong; (2) Apologize for what you did; (3) Accept the consequences of your action(s); (4) Ask God and the people you hurt for forgiveness; (5) Alter your choices in the future. See also Ken Sande with Tom Raabe, *Peacemaking for Families: A Biblical Guide to Managing Conflict in Your Home* (Wheaton: Tyndale, 2002).

details but don't overanalyze. Dwelling on the problem can cause exasperation and desperation in the person sinning and unnecessarily draw the family into further conflict. Be judicious and wise here, loving and kind remembering that 'kindness ... lead[s] ... to repentance' (Rom. 2:4).

As you take time to assess what happened, it may be advantageous to take some time out (even if just a few minutes), especially if you've pushed too hard in getting your children follow your instructions or if you've been pushed beyond your limits by them. Find a safe activity or place for your child to rest and reflect in this time-out. You might pray and read a book while you recover. You may also gain strength in contacting your spouse at times like these, or call a mentor-friend, or text an accountability partner—to ask for prayer or simply for encouragement. Then, start up again with a more realistic goal, planning something more realistic that works for your family at the time. Sometimes our expectations for our children are too lofty and unrealistic, beyond what even God expects of them. Gradually work toward a knowledge of yourself and your children that allows you to recognize when you've had enough and take that break to reassess *before* you break down.

Slowing things down will be vital for the perpetrators, too! A friend tells us that her parents and friends' parents did their best to follow Sande's rubric for conflict resolution but often their emphasis on prompt resolution and 'not letting the sun go down on your anger' was taken to an extreme and the children didn't get a chance to cool off after fights with each other. Parents were trying to talk through arguments with kids whose tempers were still hot and feelings very hurt. It was rare that apologies were heartfelt with a rushed approach. In the end, it often did more harm than good, and it would have been helpful to let some time elapse between fights and an attempted resolution, for the benefit of everyone involved. This calls for patience and the ability to live with a certain amount of tension and unresolved conflict, at least for a certain period.

2. Accept responsibility for your actions: Once you've identified what happened and what the issue is, the next step is for each of the persons involved to accept responsibility for their own actions rather than blaming others (remember Adam and Eve in the Garden). In some, if not most cases, there may be just one person responsible for the conflict, or at least one main perpetrator of the incident; however, there is often wrongdoing to be admitted on the part of more than one party in a conflict. God made us responsible agents; whether we admit it or not, we are *each* responsible for our actions. Guiding each of our children to accept responsibility for what they've done may be hard but, with appropriate balance and attention to the emotional dynamics of the situation, will go a long way toward effective conflict resolution.

3. Apologize as needed: Now that you've identified the issue and people have accepted responsibility for what they have done, it's time to apologize. Apologies should be offered voluntarily and freely rather than under coercion. Allow your children time to come to terms with what they've done and accept responsibility for their actions. If they genuinely need help guide them in formulating a meaningful, heartfelt apology. Giving them thirty seconds to apologize won't usually work. They are living, breathing, thinking, and feeling human beings who need to go through a natural process of repentance and asking for forgiveness, which takes time. As they get older, families able to prac-

> 'Sometimes our expectations for our children maybe too lofty and unrealistic, beyond what even God expects of them.'

tice reconciliation on a regular basis will develop patterns in family dynamics that restore relationships effectively, save a lot of unproductive time in arguing, and prevent unnecessary tearing down of personal self-worth and confidence of family members. Parents who apologize first set the tone for the family. Your role model of humility is so important in family dynamics. Apologize! Apologize! Apologize![8]

For example, tell your child: 'I'm sorry I was unkind to you. I was frustrated that you didn't listen to what I told you even though I asked you several times. Still, I was wrong to yell at you. Can you please forgive me?' Allow your child time to ask you questions and then help him or her verbalize their forgiveness to you if they don't know what to say. You might also explain to your child what you expect of them next time something similar happens, and guide them in understanding what hurt you, and that it also hurt God. And remember, you're still the parent. Even if you did something wrong, you'd be remiss if you didn't guide your child in the process of apologizing and restoring their side of the relationship.[9]

4. Affirm your love and affection: The last step in effective conflict resolution is reaffirming love for one another and reconciling the relationship. Give each other a hug if it comes naturally, tell each other how much you appreciate each other, and explain how the offense, however hurtful, was not intended to convey any disrespect or lack of affection. It

---

8 See Chapman, *Things I Wish I'd Known*, 118–119, who stresses the need for the following five components of a parental apology: (1) expressing regret ('I'm sorry'), (2) accepting responsibility ('I was wrong and should not have done that'), (3) offering to make restitution ('What can I do to make things right?' or 'What can I do to make it easier for you to forgive me?'), (4) expressing the desire to change ('I don't like what I did and I don't want to do it again'), and (5) requesting forgiveness ('Will you please forgive me?').

9 Again, for more on conflict resolution in families see chapter 6 below.

has often been our experience that after conflict has been resolved, the relationship can be even deeper and more meaningful than it was before. In fact, there is genuine personal and relational *healing* that results when conflict is truly and effectively resolved: 'Therefore, confess your sins to one another and pray for one another, that you may be *healed*[10] (emphasis added). Just like a fractured bone, when healed, becomes stronger than before the fracture, so a healed relationship can be stronger if the issue is truly resolved.

Managing Anger

A particularly thorny issue to deal with when it comes to conflict is anger. The Bible tells us not to sin when we're angry.[11] In fact, there's such a thing as righteous anger or indignation in the face of glaring injustice. Certainly, Jesus exhibited such righteous anger when cleansing the temple, not once but twice, when witnessing the defilement of the worship of God through commercialism and profiteering.[12] But none of us is the sinless Son of God, so even when we do witness genuine injustice, we may not always be pure in the way we respond. This is what Jesus was talking about when He called on people to take the log out of their own eye before trying to take the speck out of the eye of another person.[13]

Apart from the obvious humor, Jesus's comment reflects incredible insight into the human dilemma. Often, when we see a problem in another person's life, the reason why we're attuned to that problem is because we ourselves have that very same problem. If I'm irked by someone's competitiveness, or

---

10 James 5:16.

11 Ephesians 4:26. See further below.

12 Mark 11:15–17; John 2:13–22.

13 Matthew 7:5; Luke 6:42.

Principle	Action	Explanation
1	Analyze the issue	Ask questions. Listen. Identify the problem to find out what happened and who is responsible
2	Accept responsibility for your actions	Each person should accept responsibility for what they did rather than blaming others
3	Apologize as needed	Issue a meaningful, heart-felt apology for what you did to hurt another person
4	Affirm your love and affection	Reaffirm one's love and reconcile relationship with the other person

Figure 3: Four Principles of Conflict Resolution

arrogance, I should ask myself: Why does this other person's flaw irritate and annoy me so much? Could it be that I have the same problem? More likely than not, I do. Even if I don't, I should be careful in the way I confront the other person. God's Word tells us to restore others in a spirit of gentleness.[14] It also tells those who think they stand to be careful so they don't fall.[15]

All of this is to say that most of the time, our anger may not be undiluted, justified anger, but at best be a combination of both righteous indignation and envy or pride or some other sinful motivation. Think of the indignation of the apostles when they heard that the mother of James and John asked Jesus to allow her sons to sit on His right and on His left in the kingdom. What they were really upset about was that they didn't think of asking Him first! Sadly, this is often why we're angry with others.[16]

When it comes to parenting, it'll be important to help our children work through their anger in a way that gets to the heart of the problem. What's the cause of their anger: Is it motivated by selfishness or have they been wronged in some way? Are they angry because they didn't get their way or is there some wrong that was perpetrated that we must address? If the former, this will give us as parents an opportunity to help them come to terms with their selfishness and urge them on to a Christlike spirit (assuming they're Christians; if not, we can pray that God may expose their selfishness to show them their need for the Savior). If it is the latter, we should do everything in our power to make things right.

---

14 Galatians 6:1–2; 2 Timothy 2:25.

15 1 Corinthians 10:12.

16 Matthew 20:20–24; Mark 10:35–41.

That said, there'll be times when we're unable to undo harm that was done or bring people who have wronged our children to justice. In such instances, we'll need to teach our children to commit a situation, and other people, to the Lord, knowing that He is the judge and will ultimately call these people to account. The Bible teaches that we shouldn't retaliate but forgive those who have wronged us, following Christ's example who forgave those who put Him on the Cross.[17] Dealing with the situation privately rather than publicly and acting swiftly and without delay will lessen the tension sooner rather than later.[18] Often problems grow worse if they're not dealt with promptly because by letting the sun go down on our anger, Satan gains a foothold in the relationship. The devil can exploit unresolved anger or bitterness and sow seeds of doubt and distrust, resulting in permanently broken relationships that hinder God's blessing in our lives.[19]

But what if unrighteous anger has already been expressed? We should allow for some time to elapse with a situation that has gone awry, so the person sinning can come to terms with his lack of self-control and refresh his spirit. Reflection and repentance rarely occur immediately and sometimes require more time than you might think. Get to know your spouse and know yourself well. How do you respond under pressure and in conflict? What does it take for you to realize that you may have done something wrong? And how easy is it for you to admit wrongdoing? Learn these things about your

---

17 Romans 12:17–21; 1 Peter 2:23–25.

18 The principle of confronting others privately is enunciated in Matthew 18:15. On dealing with anger-related sin promptly, see especially Ephesians 4:26–27: 'Be angry and do not sin; do not let the sun go down on your anger, and give no opportunity to the devil.'

19 See Ephesians 4:26–27, 31; cf. Hebrews 12:15.

children, too. Once a person asks for forgiveness in the family, the person offended should learn to stand ready to forgive. The father who knows how to control his anger is a mature person who is not only fit to lead his family but also able to model such maturity in the context of the local church.[20] As a father, I should model steadiness and even-temperedness under pressure so my sons and daughters, even my wife, have a clear picture of the kind of approach to conflict we should have in our family. If I'm a model of blowing my top every time something goes wrong, they'll find it much more difficult to keep their temper in check when adversity comes their way.

Practicing Forgiveness

The beautiful thing about having been introduced to a relationship with God in Christ, and having one's sins forgiven upon repentance and faith, is that we know we're all sinners and need forgiveness. This means that we've been forgiven and are in turn called to forgive others. In genuinely resolving conflict, there's nothing like the power of actual forgiveness. Importantly, the power of forgiveness comes from the blood of Christ which was shed when He died for us and in our place on the Cross. Teach your children to treasure the power of forgiveness. They've been forgiven, and they, in turn, can forgive others. What's more, whatever wrong is commit-

---

20 Look how many of the qualifications for church leaders 1 Timothy 3:2–4 relate to self-control: 'Therefore an overseer must be above reproach, the husband of one wife, sober-minded, self-controlled, respectable, hospitable, able to teach, not a drunkard, not violent but gentle, not quarrelsome, not a lover of money. He must manage his own household well, with all dignity keeping his children submissive.' Similarly, Titus 1:7–8: 'For an overseer, as God's steward, must be above reproach. He must not be arrogant or quick-tempered or a drunkard or violent or greedy for gain, but hospitable, a lover of good, self-controlled, upright, holy, and disciplined.'

ted against them pales in comparison to what Jesus had to endure—He who lived a sinless life and was viciously vilified and crucified by sinners.

That said, the fact that Christians know the power of forgiveness doesn't mean that forgiveness will be easy. Nor does it mean that conflict resolution will always be simple. Because we're human, and because God has made us different—male and female, with various personalities, backgrounds, and so forth—there will be plenty of room for misunderstandings, hurt feelings, and other points of friction in a family setting. The other day my daughter's feelings got hurt because my son didn't tell her some piece of personal information before telling some of his friends. It took them about half an hour over lunch—with some input from the two of us—to sort out their differences. As it turned out, my son's neglect to tell his sister first was entirely unintentional, but the fact remained that my daughter's feelings were hurt. What a valuable lesson for him for when he's married! Learning how to handle conflict in the family is preparatory for living in the world and being a witness for Christ. Not only does it foster family harmony and unity, it also develops humility and growth in holiness. Therefore be thorough in working through those kinds of issues and take whatever time you need to get to the bottom of an issue to resolve it fairly.

> *'Teach your children to treasure the power of forgiveness.'*

Sources of Conflict

What are some of the major sources of conflict in families? In short, it's been our experience that there's nothing too trivial to become a source of conflict. When you live in close quarters with one another day after day, it's easy for minor irritants to turn into major grudges. In addition, sources of conflict may include the following:

- **Dealing with social media**: what age to start, what to post or not to post, family privacy[21]
- **Relationships**: issues related to dating, boyfriends or girlfriends, being left out of a social circle
- **Sibling rivalry**: alleged favoritism, parental inconsistency, territorial issues (invading or violating another person's space, not respecting their property, and so forth)
- **Disobedience**: various kinds of insubordination, challenges of parental or other authority, rebelliousness
- **Insensitivity**: boys not treating girls in a gentlemanlike manner, being inconsiderate of another's feelings, such as when they're tired or having a rough day, or girls not affirming boys and encouraging them to lead
- **Miscommunication or no communication**: unwarranted assumptions, lack of clarity, unloving words

Knowing conflict is inevitable and taking steps to ensure the proper handling of it will go a long way toward creating the kind of goodwill that is vital to resolving conflict on a day-to-day basis.

Spiritual Warfare

Thus far, we've been talking about conflict primarily on a horizontal plane as occurring between two or more individuals. Of course, that's the way we perceive all conflict, and so we typically deal with it on a human level. As Christians, however, we also know that at times the source of conflict may be supernatural. The Bible attests to the fact that God didn't merely create humans but also supernatural

---

21 See some further discussion on this in the next chapter on developing character.

spiritual beings called 'angels.' Some of the angels, the Bible tells us, subsequently rebelled against their Creator, including the highest angel, Lucifer or Satan, and his horde of demons. It's therefore possible that in a circumstance the opposition we're facing doesn't come from a mere human source but has a supernatural, evil, and demonic origin.

> 'We need to teach our children that whenever they realize that they've begun to think a thought that is unspiritual, they can cut it off and refuse to continue thinking along those lines.'

This calls for much wisdom and prayer. We've found that especially prior to major ministry engagements, spiritual opposition tends to grow more obvious and intense. The devil may try to exploit our vulnerability and weakness, or sheer busyness, by attacking us when we least expect it or are most susceptible to it. Often temptations come and are harder to deal with when we're tired after a long and exhausting day or we're vulnerable in some other way. At times, it may be a major victory or success that causes us to be overenthusiastic, unguarded, or careless, and before we know it, we've stumbled. Wise individuals will take the necessary precautions against supernatural attacks, including prayer, time in God's Word, accountability to others, and awareness of certain areas of weakness.[22]

The most detailed passage on spiritual warfare in the New Testament is found in Ephesians 6:10–18. Strikingly, the passage follows almost immediately the sections on the husband-wife and child-parent relationships in Ephesians 5:21–33 and 6:1–4, respectively. This underscores the vital connection between spiritual warfare on the one hand and

---

22 For a practical treatment, see Leighann McCoy, *Spiritual Warfare for Your Family: What You Need to Know to Protect Your Children* (Minneapolis: Bethany House, 2016).

marriage and family on the other. It's in these key areas of human existence that the spiritual battle between God and Satan rages most fiercely. At the core, the battle is for our minds: 'I am afraid that just as Eve was deceived by the serpent's cunning, your *mind*s may somehow be led astray from your sincere and pure devotion to Christ.'[23] The challenge, therefore, is this: to 'take captive every *thought* to make it obedient to Christ.'[24]

We need to teach our children that whenever they realize that they've begun to think a thought that is unspiritual, they can cut it off and refuse to continue thinking along those lines. Instead, they can pray and ask God to help them think thoughts that are pleasing to Him and that are in keeping with His will and His system of values. In this way, they'll 'not be conformed to this world, but be transformed by the renewal' of their mind.[25] Significantly, the conflicts that arise in our families may often be because of Satan's attempt to destroy God's design in our homes and to create disharmony and disunity, just as he did with the first man and woman in the Garden at the beginning.

In *God, Marriage, and Family*, I talk about three important principles for engaging in spiritual warfare: realizing that there is a spiritual battle going on; knowing the enemy;[26] and using proper spiritual weapons. As to the use of proper weapons in spiritual warfare, we've found it helpful to think of the weapons listed in Ephesians 6 in conjunction with our marriage, family, and our role as parents:[27]

---

23 2 Corinthians 11:3 (NIV emphasis added).

24 2 Corinthians 10:3–5 (NIV emphasis added).

25 Romans 12:2.

26 See, e.g., 2 Corinthians 10:4; Ephesians 6:11; 1 Peter 5:8–9.

27 The following bullet points are adapted from Köstenberger with Jones, *God, Marriage, and Family*, 161–62.

- **Truth**: Like all believers, parents and children must 'put off falsehood and speak truthfully' to one another, yet speak 'the truth in love' and thus in all things grow up into 'him who is the head, that is, Christ.' In their speech, they should make every effort not to 'let any unwholesome talk' come out of their mouths 'but only what is helpful' for building each other up 'according to their needs.'[28]

- **Righteousness**: Righteousness designates our right standing with God in and through Christ and our dealings with God and one another with honesty and integrity.[29] For this reason, it is only in marriages and families where both spouses and their children live in the power of the Spirit that God's will can be truly and consistently lived out.[30]

- **Peace**: As believers, we've been given the peace of Christ in the Holy Spirit.[31] We know that we've been eternally forgiven and that we're sons and daughters of God, that we are at peace with God, and we can be at peace with each other and act as peacemakers in the world around us.[32]

- **Faith**: As do all believers, husband and wife and their children must follow the Lord Jesus Christ in discipleship and learn to trust Him to meet all their needs and overcome all challenges and adversity. Their overriding concern should not be material needs but the extension of God's rule in the world.[33] Faith in God also entails trusting the Holy Spirit to perform His character-transforming work in their lives

---

28 Ephesians 4:25, 15, 29 (NIV).

29 Romans 5:1, 9; 2 Corinthians 5:21; Psalm 15.

30 Ephesians 5:18; cf. Romans 8:9.

31 John 14:27; 16:33.

32 John 1:12; 1 John 3:1; Romans 5:1; Matthew 5:9; 2 Corinthians 5:17–18.

33 Matthew 6:25–34.

and trusting God to lead our children to a compatible, godly spouse.

• **Salvation**: Because a married couple and children in a believing family are secure in their assurance of salvation and eternal destiny, they can truly love each other unconditionally and selflessly. The husband can provide responsible, loving leadership without abusing his authority, and the wife can trust and submit graciously to God's leading of her through her husband, so children see godly role models as they themselves hope to be married one day.[34]

• **The Word of God**: Because there is no lasting foundation for our lives apart from God's Word,[35] a married couple and their children must be committed to 'remain in God's word'[36] through regular personal and joint study of Scripture and faithful attendance of and participation in a local church where the Word of God is preached.[37]

• **Prayer**: Regular joint prayer is essential in families to 'keep the unity of the Spirit through the bond of peace.'[38] Families should make a habit of bringing their thanksgiving and requests before God and trust Him to act on their behalf.[39] In exceptional circumstances, a couple or family may even choose to refrain from sexual relations for a time of concentrated prayer.[40]

---

34 Ephesians 5:21–33.

35 Cf. Matthew 7:24–27; Hebrews 4:12–13; 1 Peter 1:23–25.

36 John 8:31; 15:4, 7.

37 1 Timothy 4:2.

38 Ephesians 4:3 (NIV).

39 Philippians 4:6–7; 1 Peter 5:7.

40 1 Corinthians 7:5.

The Bottom Line

As a realistic and relational parent, expect occasional or even frequent conflict and prepare to deal with it prayerfully, patiently, painstakingly, and lovingly. This is where the rubber meets the road. God has given us families and children to live life with. We need to welcome challenges as opportunities to grow and mature as individuals. Let's not shy away from conflict. If we fail to address and resolve issues as they arise, resentment may fester, and we'll be living with a ticking time bomb that'll explode when we least expect it and are least prepared to deal with it. With your spouse, discuss questions such as these: How can we model effective conflict resolution? How will we deal with conflict among our children? What are the conflicts that arise most frequently? Husband and wife must first learn to effectively model conflict resolution. Being able to deal with conflict effectively is one of the most important marks of realistic and relational parenting.

> *'Being able to deal with conflict effectively is one of the most important marks of realistic and relational parenting.'*

What's Next?

1. Is conflict a rare or common occurrence in your family? If the latter, what are some of the most common causes of conflict and what can you do to change that?
2. Growing up, how did you typically deal with conflict in your family? Did your parents tend to try to avoid or ignore conflict or did they acknowledge it and try to resolve it? What were some of the major sources of conflict?
3. What can you do to resolve conflict more effectively in your family, first between husband and wife, then parents to children, and among two or more children?

Part 3
Responsible Parenting

Guiding your children toward responsible adulthood

Introduction to Part 3

The third tension we encounter as parents is that of assuming responsibility for our children's development rather than adopting a laissez-faire approach and essentially leaving them to potentially harmful influences and their own devices and wisdom (or lack thereof). Now that we have learned how to parent realistically and relationally, we will see the importance of guiding and developing our children in the way they should go morally, relationally, and vocationally. We must not abandon them to the winds of the culture and evil spiritual forces. Irresponsible parenting delegates a child's development to others: non-Christian teachers, even Christian schools, immature peers, youth pastors, celebrity role models, or Hollywood. Not that these are unimportant, but let's stand up and be counted. That goes both for absentee fathers who give their best hours to their company while wife and children get the leftovers and for mothers who don't embrace their God-given responsibility of being with their children during their most formative years.

It's so easy to get sidetracked and caught up in the challenge of everyday life as a parent. You make sure your children have all their check-ups at the family doctor's office. You ensure they're not left behind socially, secure their place on a soccer or baseball team, and maybe have them learn an instrument (or two). There are countless practices and lessons to prepare for, not to mention birthday parties to attend. And for each of these parties you likely need to buy a present, or at least get a birthday card or gift card. Then, there are the various birthdays of your own children, as well as other holidays, to celebrate, including Thanksgiving (if you live in North America) and Christmas. Your social calendar is full. In fact, it's bursting at the seams!

Yet you can only kick the can down the road for so long. Eventually, *ad hoc*-parenting will catch up with you, and your children will carry on without you as their social coordinator. They may turn out to be driven, selfish, or even ruthless individuals who end up not even taking the time to take care of you or visit you in a nursing home at the end of your days! Does this sound too gloomy? We're aware of family situations where this has been the sad outcome. Therefore, it's critical not to succumb to the tyranny of the urgent and to put first things first; and that first thing, as we'll see, is character.[1]

In addition, as parents you'll be called to guide your children's education. What's the relationship between character development and education? This is too important a question not to think through carefully as parents. Your child may get a good education—but is their character being developed, and if so, in what way? Finally, as parents, you can and should have a vital hand in equipping your child for life. You can help them discern their God-given calling

---

1   Our allusion is to the classic by Charles Hummel, *Tyranny of the Urgent.* We urgently suggest you read it!

and discover their mission in life. You can encourage them to assess and exercise their spiritual gifts so they can use them in the church. You can equip them for their marriage and vocation. Seeing the end from the beginning will hopefully give you the needed perspective and purpose.

7

First Things First

Helping your child grow in character

What's Up?

Character is who a person is at the very core of their being. It affects all their relationships and accomplishments in life. Character in our children doesn't just happen; parents must be intentional and make it a focus to guide character development in their children.

As you read the following passages, reflect on the immense value of character formation in the life of your child and the role both God and parents play in this regard.

1. Read Romans 5:1–5. What engenders godly character and what is the basis for our right standing before God? What difference does that make?
2. Read Hebrews 12:4–13. What can we learn from this passage's teaching on God's loving exercise of discipline regarding developing character in our children?

The Big Picture

Many parents put a primary focus on their child's education. While education is important, such a focus on education is ultimately wrong-headed. Instead, after salvation and establishing children in their faith, parents' central concern should be on their

> 'Parenting isn't static—it's a dynamic process.'

child's character. Through children's various life stages (infant, toddler, pre-teen, teen, young adult), parents have the responsibility to set boundaries and administer discipline according to their developmental stage. Teaching about God's design for them as man or woman will provide them with a biblical framework for life. Helping them to understand the importance of purity and how to deal with social media and various other kinds of temptation will fortify them and provide a solid bulwark to keep them for a life of service. Parenting isn't static—it's a dynamic process. Parents have been given a stewardship and privilege to guide their child and to be purposeful about instilling characteristics at the right time to foster growth in character. Equipping children to make wise decisions and instilling in them a sense of integrity and responsibility will be the capstone for them to live out their ultimate true fulfillment in Christ.

The Life Cycle of Parenting

As a child encounters various challenges and opportunities, his or her character is slowly formed. From the very beginning, the tendency for many doting parents is to overindulge their child, especially their firstborn or perhaps also the youngest. If we pamper our children, however, and permit them to get their way all (or even most of) the time, we inevitably reap the consequences in the form of a spoiled, ungrateful child programed for getting his or her way. We're unintentionally training a manipulator where the child, rather than the parent, takes charge, the very opposite of fostering the character traits of submission and cooperation in the family. The stewardship is great, not only for ourselves and our children's sake, but also for the sake of family dynamics and unity, the community, and the mission of God. Therefore, it's important to stand firm as parents and to make sure *we're* parenting our *children* rather than *them* parenting *us*.

For this reason, we recommend that, as a parent, you find ways from the beginning of communicating that you, rather than your child, are in charge. This isn't a matter of trying to stifle our children's development and self-expression, or for parents to become overbearing despots. Rather, it's a sign of true, committed love, and a fulfilling of a responsible trust. As the book of Proverbs repeatedly reminds us, discipline is vital in child-rearing, and the loving parent is the one who is there to provide consistent correction and accountability.[1] So, as you move through the life cycle of parenting, from infancy to childhood to adolescence and early adulthood, the nature of your relationship with your child will change, but your commitment to building character should be constant. This is what we mean by 'responsibility' in parenting. In the short run, a laissez-faire approach to parenting may seem easier and may be smoother because there may be less conflict—but remember, *your primary goal in parenting is not to minimize conflict but rather to build genuine character.*

So, as your child begins school, is your main goal to see your son or daughter get good grades? Good grades have some value, and may be an indication of intelligence and academic ability, or at least of being able to do well within a given system of expectations, but they're not always a reliable in-

---

1   See e.g. Proverbs 6:23; 12:1; 14:24; 29:15 cf. Ephesians 6:4; Hebrews 12:5–6, 11; Revelation 3:19.

dicator of character. That was certainly the case with me as I, Andreas, was growing up. I did very well in school; so well, in fact, that some of my fellow class-mates taunted me out of jealousy. I also conformed externally to my parents' and my

> *'As you move through the life cycle of parenting, the nature of your relationship with your child will change, but your commitment to building character should be constant.'*

teachers' expectations, studying diligently, practicing piano a couple hours a day, and so forth. But in my heart, I was essentially selfish, and because my parents were pleased by my good grades and musical prowess, they rewarded me in numerous ways and held me up as a positive example to their friends and relatives.

If not grades, is it possible that your focus as parents is to promote your child's athletic success? Being a good sports parent is one of the signs of a good parent this generation is fixated on. Are you pushing them hard to excel in baseball or basketball or some other sport? You're the perfect soccer parent, present at every game, capturing memorable moments on camera and posting them on social media (only if your child's team won the game, of course), perhaps even coaching your son's or daughter's team. You sacrifice much of your time, especially on weekends, to invest in your child's recreational pursuits, and take great pains to capture every point scored, every heat won, every home run on camera.[2] Yet your child's heart may be unregenerate, his mind set on winning at all cost, his sense of identity staked on how well he does on the baseball or football field. In the end, who is going to watch all those videos? What does it matter if your son's team

---

2   In fact, it's rather common to see families with older children skip church for weekend games, and it's treated like a necessary evil.

won or lost a given game? But his character will have been formed, for better or for worse, and you won't be able to turn back the clock.[3]

Developing Character

Rather than focusing on good grades or athletic success, invest the bulk of your efforts on helping your child to develop character.[4] What do we mean by 'character'? Essentially, *character* is who a man or woman truly is in his or her heart, exemplified in what he or she does when no one's looking. Character means *integrity*, a stable core of *conviction* that isn't easily shaken by peer pressure, cultural influences, or varying circumstances. It is constant.

As you seek to shape your child's character, which values will you wish to promote? Is it serving God, loving others, developing courage and conviction, and standing up for what they believe? If so, what will your strategy be to teach and reinforce those values? Character isn't formed by default or by chance. What's more, as mentioned, children tend to imitate their parents' behavior, so we'll want to make sure that we ourselves are people of integrity.

How do we accomplish this? First, we must acknowledge we can't develop character in our children unaided by the Holy Spirit. The burden is be-

> 'Essentially, character is who a man or woman truly is in his or her heart. Character means integrity, a stable core of conviction that isn't easily shaken by peer pressure, cultural influences, or varying circumstances.'

---

3   See Jim Hamilton, 'Don't Play Travel Ball: Stay in the Rec League,' http://jimhamilton.info/2016/02/09/dont-play-travel-ball-stay-in-the-rec-league

4   See Tripp, *Parenting*, chap. 10, who takes his point of departure from Romans 1:28–32 and applies this passage to parenting.

yond measure; we can't do this work in our own strength. The Spirit must do His work in our children as they enter their own relationship with God, striving and aspiring *themselves* to be men and women of integrity and moral excellence.

Paul encourages believers to 'walk by the Spirit' and be 'led by the Spirit' and goes on to write that 'the fruit of the Spirit is love, joy, peace, patience, kindness, goodness, faithfulness, gentleness, self-control.'[5] He adds, 'If we live by the Spirit, let us also keep in step with the Spirit.'[6] Elsewhere, he urges believers to be 'filled with the Spirit.'[7] Yet in another place, he writes that 'those who live according to the Spirit set their minds on the things of the Spirit' and adds, 'If the Spirit of him who raised Jesus from the dead dwells in you, he who raised Christ Jesus from the dead will also give life to your mortal bodies through his Spirit who dwells in you.'[8]

What this catena of Scripture passages on the Spirit shows is that it is He who produces in us what is pleasing to God.

As we *walk* with Him, are *led* by Him, *live* in Him, *keep in step* with Him, and are *filled* with Him, we'll set our mind on spiritual things, and the Spirit of the risen Christ will infuse our mortal bod-

> *'It is He who produces in us what is pleasing to God.'*

ies with supernatural strength to surmount our sinful nature. In this way, we'll be able to please God and do all things through Him who strengthens us.[9] As Paul writes to the Corinthians, 'All things are lawful, but not all things are helpful' (1 Cor. 10:23). Again, the apostle strikes the balance beautifully when he urges believers,

---

5   Galatians 5:16, 18, 22–23.
6   Galatians 5:25.
7   Ephesians 5:18.
8   Romans 8:5, 11.
9   Philippians 4:13.

work out your own salvation with fear and trembling, for it is God who works in you, both to will and to work for his good pleasure.[10]

> *'As we walk with Him, are led by Him, live in Him, keep in step with Him, and are filled with Him, we'll set our mind on spiritual things, and the Spirit of the risen Christ will infuse our mortal bodies with supernatural strength to surmount our sinful nature.'*

Our children should be encouraged to actively 'work out their salvation,' trusting that God is at work in them, both to have the resolute will and the actual ability to live the life God wants them to live. This is true for us as adults, of course, and applies in the same way to our children. If you have successfully introduced your child to Christ, or they have received Him and become a child of God, their spiritual lives can be nurtured by teaching them from Scripture about the work of the Spirit along the lines of the above-cited passages.

You may even want to let them read the preceding paragraphs. You could also write these Scripture passages on a piece of paper, or in an email, and give it to them to dwell on or, better still, to memorize. The last thing we'll want to condition our children to do is live the Christian life in their own strength. This will only lead to failure and frustration, if not despair.

Instilling Virtues

In large part, helping our children develop character entails inculcating *virtues* in our children. To break down the matter in more practical terms, children's sinfulness is borne out

---

10   Philippians 2:12–13.

in several ways: they typically lack self-control and lose their temper, tend to be disobedient (or at least, shall we say,

> *'The last thing we'll want to condition our children to do is try to live the Christian life in their own strength.'*

have a mind of their own, redefining the terms of parental instruction), may be lazy or lack a proper work ethic, and are undiscerning and naïve, if not downright foolish, like we once were (if we're honest). If you want more specifics, work through this list from Proverbs. It was written to instruct young men, but the principles apply to boys and girls alike. Here's a goldmine of virtues parents can seek to instill in their young children so that when they're old they will not depart from them:[11]

- Diligence and industriousness (6:6–11; 11:27; 12:24; 13:4; 15:19; 18:9; 19:24; 20:4, 13; 21:5; 22:13; 26:13–16)
- Justice (11:1; 16:11; 17:23; 20:10, 23; 31:8–9)[12]
- Kindness (11:17)
- Generosity (11:24; 19:6)
- Self-control, particularly of speech (12:18; 13:3; 21:23) and temper (14:17, 29; 15:18; 16:32; 19:11; see also 25:28)
- Righteousness (12:21, 28; 14:34)
- Truthfulness and honesty (12:22; 16:13; 24:26)
- Discretion in choosing friends (13:20; 18:24), particularly a spouse (18:22; 31:10–31)
- Caution and prudence (14:16; 27:12)
- Gentleness (15:1, 4)
- Contentment (15:16–17; 16:8; 17:1)

---

11 The list is taken from Köstenberger with Jones, *God, Marriage, and Family*, 95–96. All Scripture references are to the book of Proverbs.

12 See the section on social justice below.

- Integrity of character (15:27; 28:18)
- Humility (16:19; 18:12; 22:4)
- Graciousness (16:24)
- Forthrightness (rather than duplicity; 16:30; 17:20)
- Restraint (17:14, 27–28; 18:6–7; 29:20)
- Faithfulness in friendship (17:17) and otherwise (28:20)
- Purity (20:9; 22:11)
- Vigorous pursuit of what is good and right (20:29)
- Skillfulness in work (22:29)
- Patience (25:15)[13]

How do you go about instilling these virtues in your children? Start with yourself. You must put a priority on developing character. You can even verbalize this by telling your children that while you rejoice in their prowess at basketball or ballet, even winning and achieving, you value even more their integrity in dealing with others (e.g. 'I liked how you encouraged the other players and didn't brag about yourself'). After a while, it may come about that they value what you value because they innately want to please you and tend to imitate and emulate your values.

The Cardinal Virtue: Humility

Let's look at the virtue that is the foundation of all the other virtues. The value of humility and practical strategies for cultivating this virtue is front and center in C. J. Mahaney's

> 'First, value character above achievements.'

---

13 For a list of virtues geared specifically toward aspiring athletes, see Pat Williams with Michael Weinreb, *How to Be Like Mike: Life Lessons about Basketball's Best* (Deerfield Beach, FL: Health Communications, 2001), who lists focus, passion and energy, hard work, perseverance, responsibility, influence, competing and winning, teamwork, leadership, respect, trust, loyalty, and character. Thanks to my son Timothy for alerting me to this book.

book *Humility: True Greatness*.[14] As Mahaney points out, the world's definition of greatness is vastly different from God's. Watch any basketball game on TV, and you'll be treated to a never-ending series of wild, chest-beating celebrations of virtually every single basket scored. One might think those players just accomplished an unprecedented feat of courage or some other rare achievement when, in fact, they merely scored a basket worth two points (or maybe three).

Just last week, during the NBA finals, my son wanted me to admit that a certain player (Kyrie Irving) was 'amazing.' I admitted that he had some nifty—even stunning—moves, but toyed with my son just a bit by acknowledging only that I thought Irving was a 'very good' basketball player. The attribute 'amazing,' I told my son, should be reserved for God (I admit I was just teasing him, but I was trying to make a point). After this went on for a little while and Irving kept scoring rather startling baskets, I eventually broke down and admitted that he was an 'amazing' basketball player, but by that time I had made my point that athletic feats on a basketball court (or other venues) are vastly overrated in the larger scheme of things.

Over against such inflated conceptions of greatness, Mahaney sets the biblical definition of true greatness in God's eyes. Consider this verse, for example, where Yahweh (the LORD) states: 'to this one I will look, to him who is humble and contrite of spirit and trembles at My word.'[15] Conversely, the root sin in Lucifer's heart prior to his fall from grace was that of pride: 'How you are fallen from heaven, O Day Star, son of Dawn! … You said in your heart, "I will ascend

---

14   Sisters, OR: Multnomah, 2005. See also the same author's *Don't Waste Your Sports* (Wheaton: Crossway, 2010).

15   Isaiah 66:2 (NASB).

to heaven; above the stars of God I will set my throne on high ... I will make myself like the Most High.'"[16]

In the New Testament Gospels, Jesus affirmed that 'even the Son of Man [Jesus Himself] came not to be served but to serve, and to give his life as a ransom [sacrifice] for many.'[17] Along a similar vein, James in his letter cites an Old Testament proverb: 'God opposes the proud, but gives grace to the humble.'[18] What these verses show is that the humble person does not exalt himself over others or even God but deflects any glory for himself to God and others in recognition of his dependence on him and them.

In view of this, Mahaney exhorts his readers to aspire to the following three things: (1) Be an example of true greatness to your children; (2) Define true greatness for your children; and (3) Discern and admire true greatness. Where, you may ask, can such true greatness be found in a person? The greatest example is *Jesus*, 'who, though he was in the form of God, did not count equality with God a thing to be grasped, but emptied himself, by taking the form of a servant, being born in the likeness of men. And being found in human form, he humbled himself by becoming obedient to the point of death, even death on a cross. Therefore God has highly exalted him ...'[19]

Other such people may include one's *parents*, certain people in our *church*, and other *unsung heroes* and *selfless servants*, people exhibiting qualities or engaging in acts that are genuinely sacrificial, humble, and unselfish. Luke tells the story of Jesus perceiving such an unselfish act during His

---

16 Isaiah 14:12–14 (though it should be noted that some question whether this reference is to the fall of Satan).

17 Mark 10:45.

18 James 4:6; cf. Proverbs 3:34.

19 Philippians 2:6–9; cf. John 13:1–17.

earthly ministry: 'And He looked up and saw the rich putting their gifts into the treasury. And He saw a poor widow putting in two small copper coins. And He said, "Truly I say to you, this poor widow put in more than all of them; for they all out of their surplus put into the offering; but she out of her poverty put in all that she had to live on."'[20] It's truly mind-transforming to ponder that a small and humble gesture can be considered great in the eyes of God. Astounding!

Mahaney recommends the following practical types of strategy for pursuing genuine humility:[21]
• Reflect on the Cross
• Acknowledge your need for God
• Express your gratitude to God
• Cast your cares upon Him
• Intentionally transfer the glory to God and refuse to take credit for your accomplishments

In addition, we can:
• Study the attributes of God[22]
• Ponder the marvel of God's grace
• Ponder the depth of our sin
• Laugh at ourselves and value humor
• Watch God at work in our own lives and in our family, church, and the world
• Encourage others, affirming and challenging them in appropriate ways

---

20 Luke 21:1–4 (NASB).

21 The following two bullet-pointed lists and questions for parents are adapted and at times conflated or supplemented from Mahaney, *Humility*, Part III: 'Our Great Pursuit: The Practice of True Humility,' 63–122.

22 Excellent resources are J. I. Packer, *Knowing God* (Downers Grove: InterVarsity, 1993); and A. W. Tozer, *The Knowledge of the Holy* (New York: HarperCollins, 2009).

Applied to parenting, ask yourself: What are my ambitions for my children? Are these in keeping with God's definition of greatness? How are you preparing and mentoring your children to move them in a Godward direction? Are you more focused on temporary recognitions or eternal rewards?

In the words of Ed Moll and Tim Chester, 'Let your child realize they're not the center of the world.'[23] We already mentioned the danger of pampering our children. What's the proper balance between loving your children and making them feel special yet not idolizing them? Virtually all parents are proud of their children's accomplishments—just look at your preferred social media site! Chances are, it's full of proud parents 'humbly' parading the accomplishments of their children. There really is no such a thing as a 'humble brag.'

Our own aspiration in this regard is twofold:

- **Try not to brag.** There are proper ways to acknowledge publicly how proud you are of your child, but we might aim to do this in as understated and humble a way as possible. In this way, we won't arouse the jealousy of others. Also, we won't inflate our child's sense of self-importance. We can certainly be grateful in our hearts to God for allowing our child to reach a milestone, and tell our child privately how proud we are of them. Of course, we'll want to make sure they know that our love for them is not conditioned by their successes or failures but that we love them no matter what. I sometimes tell my son before a game that even if he scores zero points, I'll love him the same as if he scores a hundred points, just so he knows not to connect my love for him to his performance.

---

23 Moll and Chester, *Gospel-centered Family*, 13. I have converted British to American spelling in this quote.

- **Don't overdo special occasions.** Birthdays, for example, are special occasions, but in the overall scheme are really not that important. Another year has passed. This doesn't mark an accomplishment but simply the passage of time. I think we're often too fixated on marking special occasions, and this at times becomes a burden, an expectation to live up to, especially with multiple children. Sometimes it seems almost as if birthday parties are considered a measure of whether and how much you love your kids these days! Focusing on special occasions may also perpetrate an undue focus on events and gifts, proportionately lessening the amount of attention we give to less easily qualifiable matters such as character development. Similarly, it may sound impressive that we've been married for almost thirty years, but that doesn't tell you anything about the quality of our relationship. Now please don't get us wrong here: Of course, it's great to have times when you can make people feel special and loved on their birthday and celebrate marriages. We just want to guard against any excesses here. In our experience, it's easy to go over the top. By all means, let's make our children feel special, but let's not idolize them or cause them to stumble.

Find Out What They're Good At

We believe it's vital for us to value genuine humility and to set the example for our children in this regard. It helps when your child's teachers and coaches reinforce these values as well. It's important to strike a balance here. Encouragement is important, but that doesn't mean we

> *'Try to find out what your child is good at and then encourage them to develop those skills to the fullest over time.'*

should completely ignore when our child is not succeeding in a certain task. When a boy plays baseball, strikes out, and the coaches and parents yell 'Great job!' are we sending mixed messages? How is striking out doing a 'great job'? This could be confusing even to the child. Deep down inside he knows he didn't do a good job. A better approach might be to take him aside and tell him what he could do better next time or to simply say, 'You'll get it next time.'

We should make clear that our love for our children is unconditional and doesn't depend on whether they succeed or fail in a task if they do their best and give it a genuine effort. Better still, we should try to inculcate in our children a *commitment to excellence*—to strive to excel in whatever it is they're doing. This may mean refraining from investing undue effort in certain sports or musical instruments in which they have no or little natural gifting while directing most of their energies on activities in which they stand out among their peers. Try to find out where your child is gifted and then encourage them to develop those skills to the fullest over time. That may mean sacrifice, paying for a few golf lessons, renting a violin, or whatever it takes, financially or otherwise, to help them be their best in areas in which they are truly able to make a contribution.

Help with Laziness

Does your child tend to be lazy? Most of us must work for a living, so for this reason at the very least (besides valuing responsibility as a character trait) it's an important part of parenting to instill in our children an excellent *work ethic*. One important principle here is that work typically comes before pleasure. Put differently, responsibility comes before privilege.

Does he want to watch a show or go out for ice cream? Well, has he done his homework or chores? This seems obvious, but needs constant reinforcing.

It's also important to convey that none of us always feels like doing certain tasks, even though they must be done. Did I feel like spending most of my Saturday afternoon mowing the lawn? Hardly—but it needed to be done, so I did it.

The same is true for them: Just do your geometry homework, if for no other reason because it is due tomorrow.

> 'One important principle is that work comes before pleasure. Put differently, responsibility comes before privilege.'

It's particularly vital to stress the importance of developing good study habits and a solid work ethic while our children are young because it is at this stage that they'll form habits that will stay with them for the rest of their lives.

Wisdom and Discernment

Does your child lack *discernment*? Do they say 'yes' when their peers ask them to join them in doing something that turns out to be foolish and gets them into trouble (we're sure you can fill in your own examples here)? Ann Landers (Dear Abby, an unusual source for us, we know) once wrote, 'Personality is the ability to say *yes*. Character is the ability to say *no*.' As a parent, engage your child's reasoning process, so that you can see how he or she thinks through an issue. Then, try to instill practical decision-making skills by helping them to ask questions such as:

- **Why do I want to do this?** This will get at their underlying motivation: Is it to please people? Is it to get instant gratification? Or is it truly a wise course of action that will benefit them and others and bring glory to God?

	Principle	Brief Description
1	Why do I want to do this?	Search your heart to examine your motives
2	What will happen when I decide to do this?	Determine positive or negative consequences of making a given decision
3	What are my alternatives?	If possible, make a list of all the possible available choices
4	What do people I trust recommend?	Determine if there is a coalescing consensus among trusted counselors

Figure 4: Practical Decision-Making Principles

- **What will happen when I decide to do this?** Help them to anticipate unintended consequences of their decisions, especially negative ones.
- **What are my alternatives?** This will help them to weigh the pros and cons of a given decision and help them realize that often decisions are not black and white: There may be advantages and disadvantages to most courses of action, so the best decisions are those that weigh the pros and cons and choose the best alternative.
- **What do people I trust recommend?** It's usually wise to consult with others, and to ask not just one's peers but those who are wiser and more experienced, such as one's parents or other trusted individuals such as teachers, counselors, pastors, or youth leaders.

> 'Equipping [our children] to make sensible, mature, and discerning decisions is one of the most important long-term goals we should adopt as parents.'

We've been at this with our children for many years now and have found that equipping them to make sensible, mature, and discerning decisions is one of the most important long-term goals we should adopt as parents.

Dealing with Adversity

One of the major ways in which character is formed is by dealing with various kinds of adversity.[24] If we encounter an obstacle or if things don't go our way, our natural—sinful—tendency is to whine and pout like the Israelites in the wilderness! They complained so incessantly—about the food God provided, and about the hardship of wandering through

---

24 See Mahaney, *Humility*, chap. 11: 'Responding Humbly to Trials,' 137–154, who discusses, among other things, the need not to complain, to wait quietly for God, and not to get angry.

the desert—that God barred their access into the Promised Land. Never mind that God had delivered them miraculously out of bondage in Egypt. In fact, they reminisced about the 'good old days'! They went so far as to tell Moses they'd rather be back in Egypt.[25] Talk about ingratitude!

But are we doing any better? Most of us live in unbelievable luxury compared with much of the world population, and what do we do? Yes, that's right: We whine and complain! We've found that one of the main challenges of parenting is to teach our children genuine gratitude. Better still is to embrace adversity that God allows in their lives as opportunities to learn to develop Christlike character. A true believer is yielded to God's will being done in their lives, whether this confounds their own well-laid plans or not. God never promised us that life would be easy and that we'd always get our way.[26]

Again, let's make sure that we first take this truth to heart ourselves. If I get mad when someone cuts me off in traffic when my

> '*We've found that one of the main challenges of parenting is to teach our children genuine gratitude.*'

sons are in the car with me, I shouldn't be surprised if they get mad when the umpire calls them 'Out!' when they were safe on base. It still stands out in my memory a time I was visiting with an American missionary family in Madrid, Spain and my friend Ron lost his way badly in busy traffic. Rather than give him a tough time, his wife Fran was very sweet and supportive and affirmed and encouraged him. What a wonderful role model of handling adversity in a Christlike manner! That event took place decades ago, but

---

25 Numbers 11:4–6.

26 Proverbs 16:9: 'The heart of man plans his way, but the LORD establishes his steps.'

I still remember it because it showed a demeanor that went counter to a natural, sinful tendency to complain when something goes wrong.

Self-control

Does your child frequently lose his temper? Again, first ask yourself: Are you yourself exemplifying self-control in demanding situations? Talk to your child about the importance of self-control and find ways to help him grow in this area. To some extent, emotional stability increases with age, but we should start early in helping our children develop *self-control*. When studying Paul's letters to Timothy and Titus, I was amazed to discover that the one constant quality Paul's apostolic delegates were consistently told to engender in various groups in their congregation—older men, young men, older women, young women—is self-control.[27] Self-control is also the ninth and final fruit of the Spirit.[28] Work with your children on dealing with adversity and controlling their temper. Affirm them when they take baby steps toward accepting a 'no' answer to their request to stay up late or to have brownies for breakfast. Make sure they're secure in your and God's love, so they know it's not the end of the world if they drop a ball or mess up on their recital piece. As one of our son's baseball coaches would repeat *ad nauseam*, 'Process, not results.' If you work hard on the process, results will come. We're all growing and developing in different areas, so let's help our children to set reasonable expectations for themselves, gradually setting the bar higher until they excel by God's grace and patience and self-control are increasingly built into their character.

---

27 Titus 2:2, 5, 6, 12.

28 Galatians 5:23.

Preparing Them for Mission

Leading the Family in Service and on Social Justice Issues

It's not easy for young parents—and older ones, too—to know how to guide their families in advocating social justice in a godly way. Non-Christian advocacy groups may be worldly in their methods but often highlight real injustice that the church is not always adequately addressing. Similarly, groups pushing for equality and acceptance of unbiblical lifestyles are frequently neglected by the church because they glorify or condone a sinful lifestyle. How do we show love to such people despite their sin and engage them? And how do we raise our children to *engage* instead of *avoiding* social issues that have important spiritual entailments?

Protective parents will try to shield their children from the evils of the surrounding culture in a well-intentioned effort to spare them unnecessary harm, defilement, or moral compromise. Parents certainly have a vital responsibility to protect their children from negative influences, especially during the early years when they are more impressionable and vulnerable and their character is still being formed. A long-term perspective on parenting, however, includes equipping our children to engage people in the surrounding culture with the gospel message.

Just as Jesus gathered a circle of close followers around Him for a few years, trained them in ministry, and then sent them out on mission in the world, we, too, should be diligent to take time to build up and train our children—not just to keep the gospel to themselves and keep out of harm's way. As parents our aim should be to equip our children so they can be salt and light in their sphere of influence, something they won't be able to do if they always keep others at arm's length and fail to get involved.[29]

Set Apart for God	→	**Sanctify**	→	**Send Out**
(Past Event)		(Process)		(Goal)

Before commissioning His followers, Jesus prayed for them to the Father: 'Sanctify them in the truth. Your word is truth.'[30] God had called them and set them apart; now the Holy Spirit must do His sanctifying work on them so they are ready for God to use them as His witnesses. Then they would be sent out.[31] Therefore, encourage your child to go through the process of growing in the truth of God's Word *before* they're sent out. In our home, we've found that our children began to be ready for these kinds of conversations and cultural involvement in their early to mid-teens (varying from child to child). They started asking questions, and their character began to take shape as they had to make moral choices that set them apart from their peers.

There are two opposite dangers with which parents are faced in equipping and sending out their children into the world. On the one hand is the danger of sending out your children too early, underestimating the challenges they may face. As a result, we may feed them to the lions of the culture who may devour them because they're insufficiently prepared to stand firm when they face the strong headwinds of the culture. On the other hand is the opposite danger of never sending our children out at all, whether out of fear or out of a lack of missions-mindedness. Such parents fail to recognize that we're put on this earth to be God's witnesses; they enjoy

---

29 Matthew 5:13–16.

30 John 17:17 (NASB).

31 John 17:18; 20:21–22.

His good gifts (pre-eminently His salvation in Christ) for themselves rather than sharing it with others who desperately need it.

So, then, *first*, equip your children thoroughly and responsibly with biblical truth, and make sure they're solid in character, growing in Christ, and discerning. Only *then* send them out, filled with the Spirit and part of a believing community, when you prayerfully determine they're ready. They certainly shouldn't try to go it alone but serve in company with like-minded others. In this way, they'll be accountable to those who can provide a support network and partner with them in being on mission for and with God. It's been our joy to see several young men and women who have been equipped and are now serving on university campuses or on the mission field, being powerfully used by God.

A Few Practical Suggestions

Here, then, are a few thoughts on social justice issues that may be helpful as we consider how to lead our families in a godly way. First, practicing justice in our homes, churches, and Christian organizations. Otherwise, advocating social justice in the larger culture but failing to practice it in our personal lives and circles is hypocritical and ultimately ineffective. Any meaningful impact we might have on the larger world around us will be limited.[32]

Advocating social justice is a noble and much-needed responsibility of individual Christians and of the church in

---

32 For example, churches and Christian organizations should not presume upon others to provide services free of charge but pay them fair wages. They should respect their intellectual property rather than stealing or usurping it. They should not withhold honor or recognition where such is due or uphold a double standard, honoring men but not women for serving in church-related ministry. You get the idea.

our world today. In doing so, we stand in the tradition of the Old Testament prophets, who regularly spoke out against oppression of the poor, neglect of widows and orphans, and many other injustices in their day. In this way, they served as the national conscience and called people to act out the righteousness and justice of God. As John writes in the Bible, 'if anyone has the world's goods and sees his brother in need, yet closes his heart against him, how does God's love abide in him?'[33] Jesus, likewise, called to social action, most memorably in the Parable of the Sheep and the Goats, cited below.[34] You may want to take time to read this parable with your children and discuss how you can apply it in your own context:

> When the Son of Man comes in his glory, and all the angels with him, he will sit on his glorious throne. All the nations will be gathered before him, and he will separate the people one from another as a shepherd separates the sheep from the goats. He will put the sheep on his right and the goats on his left.
>
> Then the King will say to those on his right, 'Come, you who are blessed by my Father; take your inheritance, the kingdom prepared for you since the creation of the world. For I was hungry and you gave me something to eat, I was thirsty and you gave me something to drink, I was a stranger and you invited me in, I needed clothes and you clothed me, I was sick and you looked after me, I was in prison and you came to visit me.'
>
> Then the righteous will answer him, 'Lord, when did we see you hungry and feed you, or thirsty and give you something to drink? When did we see you a stranger and invite you in, or needing clothes and clothe you? When did we see you sick or in prison and go to visit you?'

---

33   1 John 3:17.

34   Matthew 25:31–46 (NIV); see also Matthew 10:40–42; Mark 9:41.

The King will reply, 'Truly I tell you, whatever you did for one of the least of these brothers and sisters of mine, you did for me.'

Then he will say to those on his left, 'Depart from me, you who are cursed, into the eternal fire prepared for the devil and his angels. For I was hungry and you gave me nothing to eat, I was thirsty and you gave me nothing to drink, I was a stranger and you did not invite me in, I needed clothes and you did not clothe me, I was sick and in prison and you did not look after me.'

They also will answer, 'Lord, when did we see you hungry or thirsty or a stranger or needing clothes or sick or in prison, and did not help you?'

He will reply, 'Truly I tell you, whatever you did not do for one of the least of these, you did not do for me.'

Then they will go away to eternal punishment, but the righteous to eternal life.

Avenues for practical ministry abound. We can take our children to a nursing home or assisted living facility and visit the elderly, not just at Christmas or other holidays. We can work at a local food bank or clothing distribution center. We can donate items to be sent to needy children. We can visit people in prison or write letters to them. We can advocate for life, volunteer at a local pregnancy support center, and counsel and encourage those who struggle with an unplanned pregnancy. We can engage in inner-city ministry, perhaps help plant a church in the inner city or support those who do. We can help in disaster relief after hurricanes or other natural catastrophes.

These things won't happen, of course, unless we're moved by God's mercy toward us and are committed to finding ways to get involved. Too often, young people in our day—and people of all ages—are self-absorbed and look at others primarily, if not exclusively, in terms of what serves their own interests. God wants us who have received so much to give back a small portion of what we've received rather than closing our hearts toward those who are less fortunate.

Getting involved in social justice issues and engaging in social action, requires striking a proper balance between the gospel and evangelism on the one hand and helping with practical needs on the other. If we engage in social action but never mention the gospel, we've failed to help people with their biggest need of all, which is spiritual. What they need most desperately and vitally is to be reconnected and reconciled with their God and Maker in and through the Lord Jesus Christ. As we help others, we need to find ways to tell them about this good news. Also, when engaging those who live a sinful, unbiblical lifestyle, we need to balance acceptance of them as persons with not condoning their sinful acts. Increasingly, we'll be expected to embrace, even celebrate ways of living we as Christians can never support. In those situations, we'll have to take a stand and refuse to violate our conscience.

Let's make every effort to set an example as parents and to lead our children in such a way that we express our gratitude to God for what He's done for us in tangible ways toward others, both individually and as families.

Dealing with Technology and Social Media
One primary way in which character, specifically self-control, is revealed and shaped in our children is through social media. Modern technology and social media are one important reason why many parents feel that raising children is more complicated today than it has been in the past.[35]

---

35 Andy Crouch, *The Tech-Wise Family: Everyday Steps for Putting Technology in Its Proper Place* (Grand Rapids: Baker, 2017), 31, cites a Barna Research Group study that cites the following four

Yet this is not only a problem for young people; many of us parents do not have this area of our lives under control either, spending far more time on the internet than is healthy. What does this mean for the impressionable thirteen year old or seventeen year old seeking new and exciting pastimes? In our experience we have found that youth don't normally have the self-control and wisdom to deal with this area unaided by their parents. To address the challenges faced related to social media, two considerations are paramount, in our opinion: first, primarily *character*, that stems from the heart of the child;[36] and second, the need for setting appropriate *boundaries* including *accountability*.

During the tween and teenage years (in middle and high school) character continues to be formed, peer pressure is high, and values and convictions are being sharpened in the crucible of a harsh world. Self-control—such as for boys when it comes to sexually explicit images and pornography—may vary depending on circumstances. As Jesus told His followers, 'The spirit indeed is willing, but the flesh is weak.'[37] That assumes we have the best of intentions! Even so, our human make-up is tenuous and fragile. There'll be times when vulnerability and susceptibility to temptation is more acute than others, such as in evenings during down time or

---

areas as most challenging for parents today: (1) discipline; (2) time management; (3) helping children develop good moral character; and (4) monitoring technology and social media use.

36 Kristen Hatton, 'Social Media Isn't Your Teens' Biggest Problem,' www.thegospelcoalition.org, with reference to her book *Face Time: Your Identity in a Selfie World* (Greensboro, NC: New Growth Press, 2017) and other resources and ministries directed toward teen girls. See also Jacquelle Crowe, *This Changes Everything: How the Gospel Transforms the Teen Years* (Wheaton: Crossway, 2017).

37 Matthew 26:41.

when tired and defenses are down. It is vital to recognize this and plan for special protection at such times.

Talk to your children about these things to make sure that they begin to develop a lifetime of holy living in a challenging world. Knowing themselves well and being astute to the potential vulnerable aspects also of their circumstances (living, work, or school), will help them to continually adjust and set proper boundaries, guarding against temptation in the complexities of life. In setting boundaries for social media, good stewardship of time is vital. You can still affirm the positive potential for connectedness and relationship, even ministry, but expressing caution and urging wisdom and discernment is crucial. Embrace the opportunity to discuss this with your son or daughter. Ideally, they'll *want* to set boundaries themselves and will *own* these boundaries rather than having such merely imposed on them by their parents. Again, this is not a question of character *vs.* boundaries, but rather one of both character *and* boundaries!

What, then, are some helpful boundaries? One thing we've found, for example, is to be careful of otherwise acceptable social media sites that sponsor links and opportunities to connect with other questionable sites. These may expose your child to unwelcome content. One can delete these kinds of apps from their phones (though still access from personal or family monitored computers and use with discretion). You can also try to manage these through the controls and restrictions on the phone. In our experience, phones are a bigger problem than computers. This is an example of the biblical principle of *not making provision for the flesh*.[38] The idea here is that you want to teach your son or daughter to be proactive in the recognition that even where their spirit

---

38 Romans 13:14.

may be willing and they have the best of intentions, there'll be times of greater vulnerability. When those times come, they'll want to make it as difficult as possible for themselves to access bad apps, images, and sites.

Another important principle is that of *accountability*. At one point, one of my sons asked me to hold him accountable in maintaining moral purity in his internet and social media usage. We both subscribed to a monitoring site that allowed us to set boundaries and pursue accountability.[39] Of course, there are always ways around this kind of accountability if a person tries hard enough, but the point is that your son or daughter doesn't need to fight a lonely battle but rather can enlist you as his or her accountability partner and friend to help him guard his or her moral purity. What a privilege! In the case of younger children, we recommend that parents know or even retain their passwords and set appropriate limits for site usage, not only to keep them accountable but also to protect them from sexual predators. It's a known problem that children when trapped on social media are often too ashamed to tell their parents about explicit or dangerous messages, with tragic results.

It goes without saying (but because it's so important we'll say it anyway) that we should set the example in this area and ourselves seek appropriate accountability and put a high priority on guarding our own moral purity, especially in our social media and internet usage. It may help to be appropriately vulnerable and transparent with our son or daughter about some issues we've faced in this regard as well. This will encourage them and strengthen our bond with them further. They need to know that they're not alone, that we're not perfect either, and we'd love to help in any way we can.

---

39   One such website is www.covenanteyes.com. There are several others.

On a positive side, the best antidote against excessive social media use or succumbing to temptation on the internet is a strong *love for God*, being busy in *doing the Lord's work* and serving Him with reliance on the *power of the Holy Spirit*. This presupposes that our children have a growing relationship with the Lord and that they're actively nurturing this relationship through being in the Word and prayer. While they're at home with us, we can help them develop such healthy spiritual habits. Even when they're in college, we can continue to keep them accountable and encourage them in their walk with the Lord.

Above all, we should always *keep lines of communication open*—relational parenting! They should feel like they can always talk to us, especially when they need to confess that they may have slipped up in this area. While we should take sin very seriously, we should be thankful that they confide in us and assure them of God's boundless grace and forgiveness. It's amazing when we experience together the truth of 1 John 1:9: 'If we confess our sins, he is faithful and just to forgive us our sins and to cleanse us from all unrighteousness.'

Bottom line: The tech-wise family will use technology in its proper place. Andy Crouch provides the following helpful guidelines.[40] Technology is in its proper place when ...

- It helps us bond with the real people we've been given to love

---

40 Crouch, *Tech-wise Family*, 20–21 (note that a few of the phrases below are lifted *verbatim* from this book). The same author (p. 209) also recommends the following resources: Sherry Turkle, *Reclaiming Conversation: The Power of Talk in a Digital Age* (New York: Penguin, 2015); John Dyer, *From the Garden to the City: The Redeeming and Corrupting Power of Technology* (Grand Rapids: Kregel, 2011); and Art Bamford, Kara Powell, and Brad Griffin, *Right Click: Parenting Your Teenager in a Digital Media World* (Pasadena, CA: Fuller Youth Institute, 2015).

- It helps start great conversations
- It helps take care of the fragile bodies we inhabit
- It helps us acquire skill and mastery of domains of human culture (sports, music, etc.)
- It helps us cultivate awe for God's created world
- We use it with intentionality and care[41]

Social media can be a remarkable tool but shouldn't be an idol or be taken lightly. Help your child to find their identity in Christ, not through social media and approval they find in it—intensely seeking photo-ops to present themselves in a certain light, 'likes' and comments on their posts, etc. We chose to delay our sons' getting smart phones and setting up social media accounts longer than most, encouraging them to spend more of their time in wholesome activities—sports, music, outdoor fun, Christian camp and leadership development (no phones allowed), serving at church, and school with appropriate adult authority and oversight.[42]

---

41 See also the ten tech-wise commitments cited in Crouch, *Tech-wise Family*, 41–42 (some cited *verbatim*, others slightly adapted): (1) Develop wisdom and courage together as a family; (2) create more than you consume; (3) observe a rhythm of work and rest (i.e., take occasional breaks from computers and smart phones); (4) wake up and don't immediately turn on your devices, turn them off well before going to bed; (5) no screens before 'double digits' (and we would add *after* 'double digits' as well!); (6) use screens with a purpose (rather than aimlessly), and together (rather than in isolation); (7) car time (and we would add meal time!) is conversation time; (8) spouses know each other's passwords, and parents know their children's and have access to their devices; (9) learn to sing rather than merely listen to recorded music; (10) show up in person for the big events in life.

42 Regarding smart phones, see Tony Reinke, *12 Ways Your Phone Is Changing You* (Wheaton: Crossway, 2017), who identifies the following negative results: (1) We're addicted to distraction; (2) we ignore our flesh and blood; (3) we crave immediate appeal; (4) we lose our literacy; (5) we feed on the produced; (6) we become like

So, let's extol the pre-eminent role of spirituality and character in dealing with social media. And let's remember: Character matters—it always does.

The Bottom Line

It's character, parents! Focus your energies on developing character in your children. Don't worry too much about good grades or athletic achievements. They have their place, but character trumps scholastic or athletic

> 'Care more about inculcating virtues such as integrity, honesty, and selflessness in your children than being preoccupied with or blinded by external badges of honor.'

accomplishments in the end because it is a permanent, lasting fixture in all our lives even unto eternity. Winning a tournament or playing at a recital, on the other hand, is ephemeral—here today, gone tomorrow, usually quickly forgotten. Therefore, parents, care more about inculcating virtues such as integrity, honesty, and selflessness in your children than being preoccupied with or blinded by external badges of honor.[43] Let's face it, sports celebrities are often terrible role models in the way they celebrate a touchdown, or even a single tackle (not to mention life in general!).

The virtues God celebrates are the fruit of the Spirit—love, joy, peace, patience, kindness, goodness, faithfulness, gentleness, and self-control. If your child were to have to take his or her final exam in these characteristics, how would they

---

what we 'like'; (7) we get lonely; (8) we get comfortable in secret vices; (9) we lose meaning; (10) we fear missing out; (11) we become harsh to one another; and (12) we lose our place in time.

43 Understanding the scriptural balance between being and doing, character and diligence, is important. See Andreas's book on this topic, focused on scholarly excellence but also applicable to all believers, including young people, simply entitled *Excellence*. Young men particularly gravitate toward this book.

do? Would they get an 'A' or 'F' in self-control, for example, or somewhere in between? What about the other virtues on the list?[44] And what about you: How would *you* do? We know these are convicting questions. Of course, even if we do better than others in these areas, we still wouldn't have anything to boast about because it would only be due to the work of God's Spirit within us that our character and our inner disposition, and those of our children, can be pleasing to God. Nevertheless, Scripture urges us to 'make every effort' to actively pursue these virtues and to excel in them.[45]

What's Next?

1. Reflect on and discuss what degree of significance you are currently attaching to character development in your children. If you've concluded that you don't devote enough attention to character, what do you need to do to revisit your priorities and to make character development a priority?

2. How are your children dealing with adversity in their lives, such as when they are not getting their way? Do they blame others? And, how are you dealing with adversity? Are you setting a good example in this regard, and what can you do to help your children improve in this area?

3. How do you go about encouraging your children to be humble? Are you setting a good example in this regard? What's the difference between aiming high and trying to excel, and being boastful or prideful in one's pursuit of or admiration of 'greatness'? Think of concrete ways in which you could improve, whether in sports, school, or other areas.

---

44 You may even want to try to incorporate this into your schooling somehow in appropriate ways. Be creative here!

45 2 Peter 1:3–11. Andreas's book on excellence is based on this passage and discusses the committed pursuit of Christian virtues in detail.

8
A Complex Equation
Guiding your child's education

What's Up?
While character trumps education in parenting, education is also very important. Parents should affirm their ultimate responsibility for their children's education, selecting schooling options wisely, and considering the unusual spiritual and other benefits of schooling children at home.

1. Read Psalm 119:9–11. What does this passage tell you about the importance of young people being immersed in God's Word and allowing it to shape their hearts?
2. Read 2 Timothy 3:14–17. What does this passage tell you about the importance of the Scriptures in a child's upbringing as well as about the role of parents and godly mentors?

The Big Picture
Education is an all-encompassing part of our children's lives. For this reason, we believe it best to approach education as a natural process rather than compartmentalizing it. An

important dimension of parenting is passing on our spiritual and cultural heritage to our children, and understanding biblically the household's role in education. This may include language learning, family history, travel, music and instruments, communication skills (interpersonal and public), and teaching social and etiquette skills. Educating our offspring also involves learning how to teach gifted or developmentally challenged children (if you have a child in either or both categories), determining our child's learning style, and practicing the most effective methods of learning. We also have the privilege of helping our children learn how to make and save money and even how to handle their sexual urges and wait for sex until marriage. Educating our children is exceedingly important, and as parents we shouldn't want to surrender this incredible opportunity for impact and influence to anyone else.

The Value of Education

While, as mentioned, we feel strongly about the priority of developing godly character, we value education in our family a great deal. We want our children to learn about *both* God's *Word* and God's *world*. The way this is evident is in the fact that we allocate significant resources to education, both in terms of time and energy, and in terms of finance.

> 'Educating our children is exceedingly important, and as parents we shouldn't want to surrender this incredible opportunity for impact and influence to anyone else.'

It is our desire that each of our children eventually go to any university regardless of cost if that is where God leads. We've decided to trust God to provide the necessary funds if one of our children really feels drawn to a school and we believe that, all things considered, this is the best place for them to go.

Why is education so important to us? We believe that it provides a solid foundation for a lifetime of contributing to God's world and to God's mission. We also believe that education elevates a person by imparting knowledge and expertise in a field of study and, beyond this, teaches critical thinking and research skills that they can apply to every area of life. For example, I never worked directly in my original field of economics but acquired valuable research, writing, and marketing skills during my studies that have frequently proven helpful. In addition, we believe getting a good education is also good stewardship of childhood resources and time.

How are your children spending their time and resources? All things being equal (the job market is not

> '*We want our children to learn about* both *God's* Word *and God's* world.'

always predictable), our children will be better able to use their gifting and achieve their potential in appropriate vocations if they have a good education (not that 'better paying' is best, but it could be the better choice and stewardship of God's gifting!). This will help them—especially our boys as leaders—to serve God and support their family well. Getting the best possible education is also in keeping with the virtue of excellence, enabling a person to use their talents in a field of study and line of work. To be sure, some skills can be self-taught, but overall, we're firm believers in the value of formal education at their level, where students draw on the comprehensive body of knowledge in a field rather than trying to figure things out inductively. Very often in life, problems arise when a person attempts to tackle a task in which they're insufficiently trained. There's no substitute for formal education from experts in the field.

When it comes to vocational preparation, therefore, we don't believe in cutting corners. We discourage our children from going the easy way, the path of least resistance, just to get any degree. Nor should lack of finances ultimately dictate our educational choices. For one, it's not just, or even primarily, about getting a *degree*—it's about learning a given subject matter well and being equipped for life by acquiring *expertise* so you can pursue excellence. Mediocrity rarely glorifies God or serves other people well—*excellence* does.[1] So don't just substitute your hard classes in college by taking an easier equivalent at the local community college, even if that's what all your friends are doing. Prayerfully, help your child balance the demands in their lives, but encourage them to aspire to the harder thing if possible, realizing that some classes may be challenging, but if they enroll in them, and persist, they'll learn a great deal that they'll be able to use for the rest of their life.

The Place of the Household in Education: Ancient Background

Important implications for parents' role in educating children can be gleaned from descriptions of the biblical household structure paralleling ancient Jewish and Greco-Roman practices. The household was considered the basic societal unit[2] and provides a significant signpost to God's order. Rather

---

1   This is the underlying premise of Andreas's book *Excellence*. While this book is primarily oriented toward those who pursue a scholarly vocation, much in this book is applicable no matter what a person's chosen profession.

2   See the thorough discussion of the church as God's household in Paul's letters to Timothy and Titus in Andreas J. Köstenberger, *Commentary on 1-2 Timothy and Titus* (BTCP; Nashville: B&H

'Very often in life, problems arise when a person attempts to tackle a task in which they're insufficiently trained.'

than being seen as merely a matter of social convention, it was generally viewed as part of the natural order if not instituted by God Himself. Typically, the household consisted not merely of the nuclear family (made up of father, mother, and their children) but also included the extended family, such as elderly grandparents, widows, and even household servants. Interestingly, instructions regarding proper conduct in *God's* household, the church, in the New Testament, regularly include directions not only for the married couple and their children but for members of the extended household as well.[3]

Within this ancient household structure, the father, the male head of the household, functioned in a position of overall authority. He was responsible to oversee what went on in his entire household, and the members of his household were expected to follow his directions in every respect. At times, the father's authority was delegated to a manager, steward, or tutor, whose role was to manage parts of the household while remaining accountable to the male head of household. Both in terms of lines of authority and in terms of responsibilities of individual household members, then, 'Because the household was viewed as the integral societal unit, its proper ordering was essential to the health of society.'[4]

Academic, 2017), 446–482, esp. 449–465. The summary below adapts portions of this treatment.

3   See, e.g., Ephesians 5:15–6:9; Colossians 3:12–4:6; 1 Timothy 2:1–6:2; Titus 2:1–10; 1 Peter 2:13–3:9. Scholars call these portions of New Testament letters 'house tables' (or German *Haustafeln*).

4   Köstenberger, *Commentary on 1-2 Timothy and Titus*, 452.

In Paul's letters to Timothy and Titus, the household also serves as the primary metaphor for the nature of the church. In his first letter to Timothy, Paul writes, 'I am writing these things to you so that, if I delay, you may know how one ought to behave in the household of God, which is the church of the living God.'[5] As Paul's apostolic delegate, Timothy served as his deputy to ensure that God's order was followed. Paul's instructions were predicated upon the above-mentioned recognition that every member of the household has a place within the household which he or she should strive to fulfill under the overall authority, provision, protection, and guidance of its head. Instruction and education of its members was an important function of the household under the father's ultimate supervision. Not only was the household important for proper lines of authority in keeping with God's order; therefore, it was also the place where children's *education* took place.

While some of the above-mentioned characteristics of the ancient household had a cultural dimension (such as the presence of household servants), Paul's use of the household as a metaphor for the church indicates that this structure reflects God's order and has permanent significance. We see that the father is ultimately in charge of the household and that education has its center of gravity there. Also, education is ultimately the responsibility of the parents, though they may delegate aspects of their children's education to qualified tutors or stewards. Without pressing the biblical background and ancient parallels too far, we can see how the pattern we observe in Scripture is very instructive as we seek to determine the best way to educate our children today.

---

5   1 Timothy 3:14–15.

School Choice

So what's the right way to school your children? What's the best way for them to begin to learn about God's world and develop personal expertise to contribute to God's mission? While some may believe that the answer is universal—whether schooling at home, or Christian private school, or public school education—our experience suggests that the answer to this question depends on a variety of factors and may even vary for each child, and even from one year to another. We firmly believe in the importance of school choice, and certainly, as parents, we should talk and pray long and hard about where to have our children schooled. When it comes to education, we believe one size doesn't fit all.

We can share a little bit of our experience here; others will be able to give different input. To begin with, depending on the legal situation in your country or state, we encourage you to consider *schooling your children at home*. We've schooled all our children at home most of elementary, middle, and high school, though there were occasional exceptions, such as

> *'When it comes to education, we believe one size doesn't fit all.'*

when we spent a sabbatical in England or took a break in the rare year that occurred in conjunction with our children expressing a desire to 'go to school.' We're both educators, and certainly want what's best for them. So, since God supplied us with the means to do so, we chose to focus on the education of our children ourselves. It wasn't a sacrifice. It really was enriching for us as parents and has been a great joy. We found like-minded parents and families supporting each other; a community that shared resources, skills, and spiritual encouragement amongst themselves. Though at first it was an intimidating choice, at least for one of us, it was the most important choice we believe we made when it comes to parenting our children. But many questions confronted us—would we be up to the task of schooling multiple children at the same time, teaching them different subjects on various levels of education? What curriculum would we use? What about our children's social life and interaction with others? Would they all become social misfits? And what about science (we have no chemistry lab), music, sports, and other electives?

A whole avalanche of questions presented themselves as we began, especially having not grown up with any knowledge of this form of schooling. Fortunately, our state of North Carolina has a strong community of people who school at home. We attended a conference the first few years where we received invaluable input from experienced parents including being introduced to organizations that serve parents who school their children at home. We gleaned many practical tips, such as how to put together a high school curriculum, how to prepare a transcript for college applications, how to best prepare our children for college admission tests, and to get legal advice and protection if needed.[6]

We found several advantages to schooling at home in our state. First, schooling children at home provided an amazing and close *bond* between us parents and the children, and even among siblings. In a regular school setting during the child's most formative years, one usually sends their child away for much of the day and is unable to see them until their best hours have already been spent with someone else (including peers whose influence may not always be the best). Having sent a few of our children to Christian private school for a couple of their early years, we empathize. Sometimes we might have received from our children somewhat of a picture

---

6   See www.hslda.org, the website of the Home School Legal Defense Association.

of what happened that day. Most times, however, we felt we missed a sizeable portion of their experiences.

Upon offering to support the teacher or to be involved at the school, few opportunities are given, even less that involved input on curriculum choice and character development. After previously having schooled our children at home, we found the parent's role by comparison extremely minimal. When the children got home from school, they were expected to do some homework that took several hours on top of their six or seven hours at school. We often felt we might just as well have schooled them at home in the first place! So, we consider it a privilege to have guided and educated our own children primarily from a base at home and to have built upon shared experiences, taking advantage of opportunities to shape character along the way, and to become friends and advisors of our closest kin.

Of course, on the downside, you may not always have the necessary skills or knowledge yourself to teach a given subject but there are options here. I, Andreas, have never been stellar in science subjects such as physics or chemistry. Fortunately, science is one of my wife's strong suits. Praise the Lord also for competent science teachers from our church with advanced degrees (with labs in their homes!) and co-ops with qualified teachers who could partner with us and instruct our children in those areas. In our case, my wife would typically handle the core subjects—math, English, science, and history— while I would take the bulk of responsibility for the electives: languages, sports, and music. Also, I would typically prepare my children for the college admissions test (SAT) and help them with their college applications.

Second, you can *tailor* the education to a child's interests, abilities, and learning styles. Some of your children may be more academically inclined than others who are more practically oriented. You may have a particularly gifted child, you may have a child that takes longer to grasp a given context, or you may have a developmentally challenged child. If you school your children at home, no problem. You go at your child's pace, and you adapt your instruction to the way your children learn best.

Third, you have added control over your child's *curriculum*. You don't have to teach them evolution, or the virtues of same-sex marriage or transgenderism (though they should be taught about what it is so they aren't completely sheltered). You can teach your classes from a Christian world-view perspective. You can even add overtly Christian electives such as apologetics (defending your faith)[7] or hermeneutics (how to study the Bible).[8] You can also choose a curriculum that

---

7   Helping them understand the importance of world view can be extremely beneficial. A highly intelligent treatment is Timothy Keller, *The Reason for God: Belief in an Age of Skepticism* (New York: Riverhead, 2008); more basic but still helpful are Wayne Grudem, *Christian Beliefs: Twenty Basics Every Christian Should Know* (Grand Rapids: Zondervan, 2005); and Norman L. Geisler and Patty Tunnicliffe, *Reasons for Belief: Easy-to-Understand Answers to 10 Essential Questions* (Minneapolis: Bethany House, 2013). A helpful primer for high school students and their parents is Andreas Köstenberger, Darrell Bock, and Josh Chatraw, *Truth Matters: Confident Faith in a Confusing World* (Nashville: B&H, 2014), for which leader's and student's guides are available as well; for more advanced readers, we recommend the same authors', *Truth in a Culture of Doubt* (Nashville: B&H, 2014). Also helpful are Paul Copan's, *A Little Book for New Philosophers* (Downers Grove: IVP, 2016), esp. chap. 7 on 'Doubting Wisely'; Tim Albury, *Reason If You Will: How to Answer Questions Regarding Faith* (n.p.: Rainer, 2014); and William Lane Craig, *On Guard: Defending Your Faith with Reason and Precision* (Colorado Springs: David C. Cook, 2010; I worked through this with one of my sons, though the later chapters got a bit technical).

8   Teaching your children how to study the Bible is a wonderful privilege and responsibility. I was privileged to work through a book

integrates various subjects, such as English literature, world history, and Bible. You can include subjects not always taught in public or other schools, such as speech and debate, logic or Latin. In our family, we've greatly enjoyed our children taking part in several speech and debate tournaments, and my husband has taught Latin to a small group of children— including our own—in our home.

Fourth, you have additional *flexibility*, which is especially helpful if you, like us, can travel and minister at various places during the year. In addition, you can use your travels for education purposes (field trips!). Over the years, we've traveled through much of North America and part of Europe, which in large part was possible because of added flexibility through schooling at home. Occasional field trips (local as well) are invaluable because they provide real-life encounters and show the relevance of what our children are learning in the home classroom. I can't tell you how many times we'd read something in a textbook and I could remind my child about our travels. Stimulating discussions have ensued in our family about the Spanish-American conflict at the Alamo; the flourishing of the arts in the Middle Ages

---

I wrote with Richard D. Patterson, *For the Love of God's Word: An Introduction to Biblical Interpretation* (Grand Rapids: Kregel, 2015), with my sons. An excellent book to use with daughters is Jen Wilkin, *Women of the Word: How to Study the Bible with Both Our Hearts and Our Minds* (Wheaton: Crossway, 2014). A solid book on inductive Bible study is R. Alan Fuhr and Andreas Köstenberger, *Inductive Bible Study: Observation, Interpretation, and Application through the Lenses of History, Literature, and Theology* (Nashville: B&H, 2016). Many questions will be answered by Robert L. Plummer, *40 Questions about Interpreting the Bible* (Grand Rapids: Kregel, 2010); and Greg Gilbert, *Why Trust the Bible?* (Wheaton: Crossway, 2015). Another useful tool is a good Study Bible. Give your children one and then encourage them to consult it when they're reading their Bible or as questions arise. We recommend the ESV Study Bible, CSB Study Bible, and Zondervan NIV Study Bible, among others.

in Venice, Italy; and a considerable number of historical and educational topics at various times: Stratford, England and Shakespeare; Geneva, Switzerland and the Reformation; geology/evolution and the Grand Canyon; the list goes on and on. In keeping education interesting, even fascinating, field trips can make an enormous difference though we understand it may not always be economically or otherwise feasible for families to travel all over the world.

We could go on to list further advantages of schooling children at home, but as you can see, whether you're able or find it advantageous to do so or not, there are many reasons why you might want to consider assuming the responsibility for the education of your children. In your role as a parent, if you choose to entrust the care or education of your children to someone else, make sure their values match your own as closely as possible, or you'll have to undo some of the negative influences and consequences that will likely result.[9] Schooling at home is not for everyone, of course. In any case, start thinking early about what your values are regarding your children's education and how to best ensure that your values carry the day. Unless you're *intentional* about your children's education, someone else—possibly with values different than your own—will call the shots, and you may not always like the results.

Responsible parents will make every effort to make an informed and prayerful decision regarding their children's education. Find out what all your options are. There are con-

---

9   This lesson was painfully reinforced for us just recently when we allowed one of our children to go on a church trip that, as it turned out, was supervised only inadequately by a young, inexperienced youth leader and a college-student intern. We're still in the process of cleaning up some of the resulting mess, though we learned a valuable lesson.

	Benefit	Brief Description
1	Create close bond between parent and child, siblings	Spend invaluable time with child teaching them subjects in area of own expertise
2	Tailor education to individual interests, abilities, and learning styles	Greater individual attention, more effective education
3	Control over child's curriculum	Offer subjects not taught at public school, classical curriculum, values, Bible, etc.
4	Flexibility	Opportunity for field trips, extracurricular educational opportunities, travel

Figure 5: Benefits of Schooling Children at or from Home

stantly new options available, so try to stay current. Realize that what may be right for one child may not be best for another. We've always taken it one year at a time, one child at a time though our preference was to coordinate all the children's schooling. Also, while we personally believe that educating our children at home was the most valuable and strategic choice we made in terms of parenting, we know that there are genuinely some circumstances that lend themselves to other school options that might be best for a given family or child: that may be public school, Christian private school, or some other arrangement (but, remember, again, you'll be giving up a good deal of parental presence, authority, and protection in those cases).[10] It's up to you to determine what to do in any given year with a given child, keeping in mind the larger foundational values sketched out above that should guide your specific decision-making regarding your child's schooling. Also,

> 'Responsible parents will make every effort to make an informed and prayerful decision regarding their children's education.'

we realize that the educational scene (including the legal situation) will vary considerably depending on the country, state, or educational district where you live.

Life Experiences as Education

Education is more than just head knowledge acquired from book, or at school (if you don't school at home). It is all-round preparation for life—learning about personal giftedness and finding one's place in God's world. This includes academics but should also involve real-life experience gained

---

10   Private schools sometimes offer classes and oversight as an 'umbrella,' which is helpful in states less friendly toward schooling children at home (such as California).

working with other people and serving in the community. If you school at home, this is more easily and thoroughly incorporated in your days together.

One of our sons, now a junior in college, spent his 11th and 12th-grade years being schooled at home (among other years)—which in his case involved taking various classes from experts at quality co-ops once a week, in different subjects, from a variety of teachers, and completing work and assignments at home under the direction of parents. In addition, he found time to work part-time in various capacities—assisting an elderly gentleman with dementia several times a week, working at a Clubs-and-Clinics track-out program at a local Christian camp, and even managing a booth at the North Carolina State Fair. He had lots of fun in his last two years in high school (though he worked hard in his academic subjects), and even made quite a bit of money, so much so that he was recently able to use his savings to buy his first car.

We can't take too much credit for our son's 11th and 12th-grade years. We tried to guide him, but ideally by that time a young man should be equipped to be an active participant in designing his own education. In this way, starting college, he became equipped to make good choices in course selection and in choosing professors as well as finding an appropriate major.

Remember, as in all parenting, things will not always go perfectly. We're not perfect and live in an imperfect world. We'll certainly make mistakes. Consequently, we'll have to make appropriate adjustments along the way. For example, we gradually realized that a curriculum we were using was strong in classical education but weak in math. Accordingly, we tried to find some ways to boost our child's math education. Regarding sports, one year one of our sons played on a travel team. While it was an exciting and in some ways even exhilarating season, we concluded that in the end it was not worth the sacrifice of missing quite a few Sundays in church, and setting what we considered to be a terribly wrong precedent in the long haul. We're very glad we made this adjustment, and God provided some more wholesome substitutes that don't force us to neglect what's more important—our son's spiritual development.

The Mosaic of Education

As we mentioned earlier, a significant part of parenting is passing on our spiritual and cultural heritage to our children. While we don't have the space to go into detail here, let us just mention some of the possible ingredients in the educational mix you'll likely want to provide for your children, whether you school at home or elsewhere, including some tips on preparing for college admission.

First, know what the minimal requirements are for your state (or country) for your child's education. Determine if your child is likely to be on track toward college, and if so, learn what the general college requirements are, as well as those for specific universities they may aspire to attend. Requirements vary. You need to know your child and their personal and academic bent. Guide them individually here. The College Board was helpful for us in determining an appropriate high school curriculum for college preparation.[11] The high school transcript in the US is the only level of education that is adjudicated for college admission in the United States, so any academics prior to this primarily serve the purpose of giving your child a solid academic foundation for high school. Therefore, there is a lot of freedom in the school years before high school; use this area of discretion

---

11   In the USA, refer to www.collegeboard.org for more information.

to your child's advantage, balancing end goals of life, faith, marriage, family, *and* career. In this way, your child will be grounded and well-rounded spiritually, academically, and practically. If your child is academically gifted, they may be able to get a jump on science, math, and other subjects if you plan their early education accordingly. They may even be able to take AP courses and earn college credit through a successful performance on final exams.[12]

In addition to covering core courses for your children's education, you'll want to encourage them to learn one or more foreign languages. Of course, make sure you start with teaching them your native language well, such as English for most of you reading this book. Too often we've found that young people are weak even in the basics of English grammar and syntax (sentence structure).

When it comes to learning *foreign languages*, there are several wonderful options available today that weren't available even only a decade or two ago.[13] In our experience, it's never been easier to learn a foreign language. There are so many benefits to learning another language and traveling to other countries. Your children's heart for others in other countries will be stirred and their horizons be expanded. They will see their own lives in larger perspective and can relate better to people who are different than them. Learning

---

12 See www.academy.hslda.org for one example of quality high-school courses for 9th grade through 12th grade including AP courses for students schooled at home. These courses consist of a live online-class meeting led by a qualified teacher each week, with follow-through in the home. One additional benefit of such courses is the flexibility granted for students and families involved in intensive extracurricular activities such as debate, sports, or traveling ministries.

13 For example, one of our sons has benefitted greatly from a four-year German curriculum developed by a native German speaker, Mr. Haegele, in Cary, NC.

a foreign language will reinforce their grasp of their own native language. It'll help them read works written in that other language and perhaps even communicate with those in other cultures. Even if they can't *speak* the language, they'll still appreciate other customs and people in other cultures—their musical styles, their special dishes, and so forth.

I still remember driving through Europe with our family (a wonderful privilege since I myself grew up in Vienna, Austria) a few years ago and reading a book on *etiquette*. It was very intriguing to all of us—including our children—that customs vary significantly in different European countries. Later during that same trip, when a German colleague had us over to his house for dinner with his family, he pointed out to our children what constituted proper table manners in their context (saying 'Guten Appetit!' before you start, don't switch your fork and knife back and forth, and *never* use your hands!). How eye-opening! These kinds of experiences show how some aspects of our own culture are relative, and customs in other cultures are equally legitimate yet different. This realization can engender respect for others and help young people appreciate the diversity of the various groups of people in our world.

Not only does education include language learning, it may also include mastering a *musical instrument*. Whether you're gifted musically or not, most of us enjoy listening to music and have distinct tastes and preferences in musical style. In addition, some of our children may have special abilities with music; we should encourage them to develop those for the glory of God and the enjoyment of all of us. In fact, it's not just being able to play an instrument that is worth pursuing; one thing I, as a parent, appreciate is the character formation that accompanies taking music lessons. Over time, a young person acquires a certain amount of discipline by having weekly music lessons and by practicing pieces on a daily (or almost daily) basis. Music education is a wonderful gift for all students in our opinion. It can also be a lot of fun to play in an orchestra or a band and see how one can make beautiful music together with others.

The same benefit of discipline can come from playing *sports*. In our family, we've been greatly blessed with coaches who look at sports as a means of discipleship of young men. These coaches had genuines heart for the spiritual development of their players. One coach has matched up more mature players with less mature ones as 'accountability partners' as part of a mentoring program, also hosting regular Bible studies and prayer times. The young men on the team are encouraged not to wait until after college to take an interest in spiritual things but to accept responsibility for becoming strong Christian men now, as young men. In an age and culture where we too often baby our children and are too soft on them, we appreciate a coach who is rigorous in terms of physical discipline as well as in spiritual accountability. Not that we should delegate this role entirely to a coach or teacher, but it helps to partner with coaches, other parents, and role models who can be allies with us in mentoring and discipling our children.[14]

Practical Tips

Space doesn't permit to fully cover other important aspects of our children's education, but we'd at least like to share a few additional ideas.

Regarding your *spiritual heritage*, make sure to tell your children how you came to know the Lord. Share your

---

14 Conversely, we once chose to attend another church because we felt some of the key pastors were not the kind of role models we desired for our young boys.

testimony with them! Part of this, as mentioned already, may be to travel. Show them where you grew up, and tell them about some of the things you did as a young person and how and when and where you met the Lord.

Part of their education and socialization may also be to teach them about their *family history* and *ethnic and cultural heritage*. Share about family traditions and about some of their ancestors. In this regard, you could engage in genealogical family research together. In our case, they have an Austrian father and a Canadian mother, and our mothers are German and British, respectively. We even have family members who live in Australia!

Also, put special emphasis on helping your children develop strong public and private *communication* and *interpersonal skills*. This will be aided by reading and developing an active vocabulary. It can also be enhanced by participating in an informal or formal speech and debate program as mentioned above. Teaching your children social skills and etiquette, in a way that helps them to act with kindness toward those around them, will be beneficial to them and anyone they meet. The first time we signed one of our children up for a local cotillion program (where young people learn social etiquette), he—uncharacteristically, for him—had a very strong adverse reaction. *No way* was he going to do this! We almost literally had to drag him to his first lesson kicking and screaming (OK, I'm exaggerating). God has a sense of humor, however, because that child since did a complete 180 and has served as an assistant instructor for several years, eventually having a ministry amongst the young men he met there.

Delegating sex education outside of the parents' realm, such as the public school, is a questionable decision for any Christian parent. So is entrusting discussions regarding purity to the youth leader or other pastors in the church (though hopefully they will be supportive of your views in their biblical instruction in this area that they give to those under their leadership)! So, you must take initiative in your home to set the stage for their lives in these ways.

We talked about the 'Big Three'—money, sex, and in-laws—earlier. Don't wait until premarital counseling of your child to tackle these vital topics. Some parents are also rather secretive about their *finances* (others are just disorganized). Ideally, try to find appropriate, and if necessary, discreet ways to draw your children into the way in which you manage your money and to mentor them in these areas. For example, you may establish a budget organized by categories (housing, food, clothing, education, entertainment, and so forth) and share it with your children. This will help teach them the value—and limited availability—of money and hopefully help them be more appreciative and grateful for the way in which God provides for your family.

Also, you may want to consider starting them on an age-appropriate allowance. We've seen both extremes—too much or too little. Again, be careful not to pamper them; they can begin to see the value of earning some of their own money if you don't completely cover their wants; they can also see the value of family dynamics and community if they are encouraged to continue to contribute at home with chores, without an expectation of payment (mowing the lawn, making a meal, painting the fence, etc.). Find the right balance for your child. As they grow older, you can encourage them to find part-time employment locally. Help guide them in making wise decisions on how to spend their money allowing them gradually to make their own choices. They'll learn from their successes and also some failures. Later still, you can help them research how to invest their money and guide them in their financial decision-making.

Make yourself available to teach them about *sex*.[15] Sex is one of God's most extraordinary gifts, to be enjoyed exclusively in marriage. Prepare your child beforehand for these kinds of talks from others. We've found that the age of twelve is generally an appropriate time to do this, before children enter the teenage years. That said, if you try to initiate conversation and your child is disinterested, you may want to wait until he or she is ready. Alternatively, if they're asking questions earlier, take the opportunity to talk about the subject at the level at which your child is interested and ready to address it.

In a non-judgmental way, make sure they know they can always come to you and talk to you about their struggles in this area. Be personal and share (appropriately) some of your own struggles with them and offer advice on how to guard against succumbing to sexual temptation. We both love the Passport to Purity™ and Passport to Identity™ resources and have gone through these with our children.[16] We continue to pray that God will spare us seeing our children fall into grave sexual sin and that He will guide them to pursue relationships that honor Him.

The Bottom Line
Within the context of character development, place considerable value on your child's education. Education is very crucial, though not all-important! Be responsible as a parent in this crucial

---

15 This area overlaps with character (sexual purity), which we've covered in the previous chapter, and has also implications for 'courtship' and dating, which we'll cover in the next chapter. Please see the discussions there. See also chapters 2 and 4, entitled respectively, 'Marriage and Sex' and 'Reproduction and Parenting,' in Köstenberger with Jones, *Marriage and the Family*.

16 These resources were developed by and are available from FamilyLife under the leadership of Dennis and Barbara Rainey. Highly recommended! A bit older but still helpful is Stephen O. Watters, *Real Solutions for Overcoming Internet Addictions* (Vine, 2001).

area of your child's life. Establish spiritual and educational values and goals, and choose the most appropriate form of education for each of your children at every juncture of their development. As you do so, there is freedom to partner with others but assume ultimate responsibility for their education. As your children grow older, involve them increasingly in this decision-making process as part of equipping them for life. In the last chapter of this book, we'll talk some more about what it means to equip your sons and daughters for life: helping them to discover and fulfill God's mission for which they were created, and guiding them in their pursuit of their God-given calling.

What's Next?

1. How important is your children's education for you? And what type of school do you prefer: public school, private school, schooling at home, or some other setting, and why? Are there circumstances such as finances or expediency that influence your choice?

2. Has this chapter affected your view on what education is and how you can best fulfill your role as a parent concerning your children's education? Do you believe parents' spiritual duty to educate their children is part of fulfilling their role as parents?

3. How can you increase your education-mindedness in your family? How can you inspire in your children a greater joy of learning and discovery? How can you genuinely accept responsibility for your children's education regardless of the type of school you choose?

9
Equipping for Life
Spiritual gifts, mission, marriage, and vocation

What's Up?

Parenting takes place at the intersection of three missions that encompass the parent, the child, and ultimately God. The mission of parenting—bringing children into this world and raising them to love and serve God—involves equipping children for their particular mission in life and takes place within the larger scope of the mission of God: raising up a people who love and serve Him for His glory! As parents help their children find their place in this world, they can assist them in determining their natural and spiritual gifting, guide them in pursuing a potential career/calling, and aid them in charting a wise course of action in life and significant relationships.

1. Read Romans 12:1–2. What can you learn from this passage about decision-making and the will of God in a person's life?

2. Read Ephesians 5:18, 21–33. How can you teach your children about the distinctive roles and missions of husband and wife as you prepare them for marriage?

The Big Picture

One of the most exciting privileges of parenting is helping guide our children toward their mission in life. As parents help their children discern their calling from God and discover their natural and spiritual gifts, the children can learn to serve the Lord in their church and move toward choosing a life vocation. Helping them in this way requires a listening approach to your child and to God. What are you child's strengths? What is the best way for them to pursue their calling? How should they go about choosing a life partner? How do we guide them to discern God's will for their lives?

The Mission of God

Rather than focusing primarily on God's individual mission for your child—or yourself—it is instructive to start with God's own mission. Once we have a clear picture of God's mission in this world, we'll be able to see more clearly how we each can join God in His mission. So, what is God's mission? This question entails biblical theology, that is, a study of the storyline of the Bible to discern God's overall plan.[1] Like

---

1   An appealing resource for younger children is Kevin DeYoung's, *The Biggest Story: How the Snake Crusher Brings Us Back to the Garden* (Wheaton: Crossway, 2015). More advanced are T. Desmond Alexander, *From Eden to the New Jerusalem: An Introduction to Biblical Theology* (Grand Rapids: Kregel, 2009); Craig G. Bartholomew and Michael W. Goheen, *The Drama of Scripture: Finding Our Place in the Biblical Story* (2nd ed.; Grand Rapids: Baker, 2014); and Preben Vang and Warren G. Carter, *Telling God's Story: The Biblical Narrative from Beginning to End* (2nd ed.; Nashville: B&H, 2013). A useful tool for Bible study is Scotty Smith and Michael Kelley, *Ventures in God's Unfolding Story*, Foundations Curriculum (vol. 3, books 1 & 2;

a symphony, it is helpful to view the story of Scripture as unfolding in four movements: *Creation, Fall, Redemption,* and *Consummation.* Within these four movements, consummation corresponds to creation, and redemption corresponds to the Fall.

'In the beginning,' the Bible tells us, 'God *created* the heavens and the earth.'[2] The Bible presupposes God's eternal existence. Those who don't believe in God should contemplate that there is abundant evidence in our world for the existence of a Master Designer and Creator. What's more, not only did God create the heavens and the earth in general, He created you and your children specifically. By getting married and starting a family, you're already fully engaged in God's mission; for the Creator charged the first couple, who had become one flesh in marriage, to multiply and fill the earth. Thus, marriage and family are a central and integral part of God's purposes for humanity generally and for each of us individually.

In exploring God's mission, people in the church often start immediately with the Great Commission which is found at the end of the Gospel of Matthew.[3] The risen Jesus's commissioning of the eleven apostles as *representatives of the church* is indeed a climactic moment in Jesus's mission and vital in understanding His purpose for His *new messianic community, the church.* However, if you *start* there, we believe you're missing some important dimensions and entailments of God's mission in this world that affect you and us very directly. Specifically, you're missing the fact that the Great Commission isn't just addressed to followers of Christ

---

Brentwood, TN: Brentwood Baptist Church, 2015).

2   Genesis 1:1, emphasis added.

3   Matthew 28:18–20.

generically but to these followers specifically as *husbands* and *wives* and as *fathers* and *mothers*. Being a Christian will play itself out in community, in teamwork, and in the *local church* by merely living out His design for you as man and woman.[4] In this way, the Great Commission builds on God's original purpose for creating humanity in the first place, extending God's glory through the earth as man and woman partner in the procreation of children and thus exercise dominion on His behalf.

At this point in this brief overview, we must introduce the second movement in the biblical story, the *Fall* of humanity. If the Fall hadn't occurred, God's purpose for marriages and offspring would have resulted in families spreading the knowledge of the Creator to the ends of the earth by extending and reflecting His image and likeness throughout the earth. However, the Fall introduced a major complication—to put it mildly—into the divine mandate for humanity. When Eve took of the forbidden fruit and Adam followed suit, the result was that now all of humanity was implicated, and all are now considered to have sinned and fallen short of the glory of God.[5] Think of it as a broken mirror. You can still look at it and see your face, but your facial features will be distorted, and you'll need to get a new, unbroken one, to see the true image. You just can't adequately fix a broken mirror.

Something similar happened to humanity when Adam and Eve transgressed God's command. They could no longer fulfill God's original mandate for them—which wasn't merely to marry and have children (though this continues imperfectly in our world with believers and unbeliever alike), but originally was an institution created to *reflect His image*

---

4   Again, we refer you to our book, *God's Design for Man and Woman*, for a full description of God's mission for man, woman, and family.

5   Romans 3:23.

and glory. Marriage and family can only now reflect, like a broken mirror, imperfectly. In fact, God expelled the first man and woman from His direct, immediate presence in the Garden; so now sinful human beings could no longer live in God's presence but were instead separated from Him. What makes matters worse, there's nothing they (or we) could (can) do to save themselves (ourselves) from this exceedingly serious predicament. With the apostle Paul, we cry, 'Wretched man that I am! Who will deliver me from this body of death? Thanks be to God through Jesus Christ our Lord!'[6] Once humanity had rebelled against God, people had become impotent to save themselves and fulfill His mission. The next move was up to God.

And, thank God, He *did* move, albeit very slowly, in what constitutes the third movement in the biblical story. Over the course of Old Testament history, God gradually exposed human sin—especially in the universal flood—and then chose individuals in and through whom He would act *redemptively* in the Messiah. He chose a man named Abram (later renamed Abraham) and promised that in him, through his descendant, all the nations of the earth would be blessed.[7] Later, He chose Moses and appointed him to lead His people Israel out of bondage in Egypt and to give them the Law, communicating His specific expectations (the standard of righteousness) in the interim between the Fall and the coming of the Messiah.[8] Later still, He chose David to rule His people Israel as a caring shepherd, the forerunner of the Messiah, who would be called the 'Son of David.'[9] Then, in

---

6   Romans 7:24.
7   Genesis 12:1–3.
8   Exodus 20; cf. Deuteronomy 5.
9   See esp. 2 Samuel 7:13–14.

the 'fullness of time,' God's appointed time, God sent His Son, the Lord Jesus Christ, born of a woman, born under the Law, to redeem those who were under the Law, by dying on a Roman cross for the sins of the world.[10] At this point, we're given the opportunity to be brought back into the presence of God and to experience reconciliation and deliverance from our eternal separation from Him. This rescue is available only through Jesus, 'the way, the truth, and the life.'[11] All we need to do is to accept God's gift of salvation and trust Christ, and Him alone, to be our Savior and Lord. It's as if God were saying, 'Turn around. Face me. Now move toward me.'[12]

This is the movement in God's story—God's mission—in which we live out our lives and equip our children to do so today. The fourth and final movement, the *consummation* of this story, is yet to come. So, how does parenting fit into the biblical story? What does it have to do with the very mission of God?

Simply put, our mission is this: As Christian parents, we've been reconciled to God and are again able to live in God's spiritual presence through Christ and the Holy Spirit who lives in us. We're part of redeemed humanity, which is again enabled to make God known and to reflect His glory on this earth. How are we to do this: as generic individuals? No—as redeemed men and women who as married couples reproduce and procreate children who in turn need to be reconciled to their Creator and be taught about the wonderful salvation God provided when He sent His beloved Son to die for us on the Cross.

---

10 Galatians 4:4.

11 John 14:6.

12 Ray Ortlund's paraphrase of a statement by the renowned British theologian J. I. Packer, author of *Knowing God*.

Our mission in making disciples—God's mission for us—starts in the home. Our first disciples should be our own children! If we neglect to prioritize this vital stewardship of discipling our children, little else we engage in will matter much for eternity. If we're not committed to making our families and homes a place of mission, then something is off balance. Not that we should stop there—rightly understood, we should be 'Great Commission families,'[13] united in purpose, bonding together in love, embracing and fulfilling God's purpose for our lives individually and jointly, and consider ultimately *the church* is the family of God made up of those who are spiritually brothers and sisters in Christ.[14] This constitutes a full-orbed—rather than truncated and reductionistic—understanding of the mission of God and of the way in which we participate in it.

The Mission of Parenting

Parenting, therefore, is more than merely training and disciplining your children for a productive life on earth. It's more than taking them to baseball practice, dance recitals, and music lessons. It's even more than taking them

> 'Our mission in making disciples—God's mission for us—starts in the home.'

---

13 See Daniel Akin, 'Building Great Commission Families,' http://www.danielakin.com/wp-content/uploads/2015/12/ETS-2015-Building-Great-Commission-Families.pdf

14 See 1 Corinthians 7:6–7, 25–35 for the role of singles in God's mission. See also Jesus's words in Matthew 19. There are some specially called by God to remain unmarried so they can serve Him without the added responsibilities that come with being a spouse and a parent. This unique and select calling does not compromise God's original plan for man and woman but serves as a special service to the church and is for a limited group of people. It also anticipates the final state where all people will no longer marry but be like the angels.

to church and memorizing a few (or plenty more) Bible verses (though that's a great start). Parenting, rightly understood, is *mission*. In fact, it's part of *God's* mission for the world, and specifically for you and your spouse. In bringing children into this world and in raising them to love and serve God, you are part of God's mission.

As mentioned, this involves nurturing Christlike character in our children rather than merely giving them an education, no matter how excellent. It also requires that we take a long view of God's purpose for them, so we won't get caught up in the daily minutiae but parent *responsibly*, with *purpose* and perspective. It requires acknowledging and adhering to the God-ordained roles for men and women, so that the mother is free to nurture her children and care for them while the father is encouraged to lead and provide for his family.

> 'Parenting, rightly understood, is mission ... *In bringing children into this world and in raising them to love and serve God, you are part of God's mission.'*

Helping Them Find Their Place in This World

That said, God made each of us unique, with a certain set of gifts and a special calling. Like a Christmas present, this calling and these talents (and spiritual gifts upon conversion) are wrapped in a neat (or not-so-neat) little package which is your child. Usually we've found in our own lives that what a child gravitates to early on ends up being central to their ministry and vocation later. Over the years, try to help them unpack that gift. Observe your child and see what he or she is good at. I remember one boy on my son's baseball team who seemed to have difficulty catching a ball and running the bases. I realize you can certainly teach a kid to catch a baseball over time, but it occurred to me that perhaps baseball wasn't what that boy was particularly good at. (Of course, he may still have enjoyed playing the game, and he certainly got some great exercise.) At the same time, all of us are good at *something*! The joy is finding out what that is and then developing that gift, and we can help our children to excel in this.

When our oldest was only a little girl, she was a voracious reader who would lie on our living room couch for hours and read one book after another from start to finish. By the time she was in high school, she had read hundreds of books, all at her own initiative. Her vocabulary was expansive, and her grasp of English literature advanced. In fact, she would outdo her dad in spotting typos on billboards, church signs, and in books she read. In college, she majored in journalism with a focus on public relations. After several publishing-related internships, she worked for a time in children's book publicity for a large publishing company. We share this because you can see that there were some rather obvious indications early on as to what our daughter enjoyed doing.

Or take our other daughter as an example. As she grew and developed as a teenager, she showed an interest in healthy eating. She started reading about nutrition and discovered its value for physical well-being. She encouraged us to buy healthier food and as part of her exploration tried out some vegetarian menus. This wasn't part of any class or external influence, it was motivated by what was in her heart. She entered college in a generic field, not sure if she could handle the sciences, but then switched to nutrition, trusting God to enable her to succeed. She is now pursuing graduate-level work in Human Nutrition with hopes to help mothers in the field of maternal infant and child nutrition, focusing on the effects early nutrition has on children's development and long-term health.

Our oldest son was often involved in organizing things: leading in ministry for young children at the local Christian camp, fundraising for the Red Cross, and managing a friend's business for the State Fair. He is now studying for a BA in Business Administration with a concentration in Marketing.

Things won't always be as simple and straightforward, but if we're observant, we'll often be able to help our children discern their passions and drives in life and assist them in developing their gifts. Being able to find a vocation that you're good at and that you enjoy doing will be a tremendous blessing for yourself and those around you.

These, of course, are ongoing stories. It's our hope that God will use our daughters' education and passion in the context of their families and in ministry to other families as well and that our sons will lead in ways that are helpful for the body of Christ in their areas of expertise. Our youngest is still at home and is 'majoring' in basketball! He is also a gifted musician who plays piano and violin very well. We're waiting to see how God will develop him and in what direction He will take him in the years to come.

> 'Every child has his or her own experience in life with God and pace of growth in maturity.'

Natural and Spiritual Gifts

Speaking of giftedness, both of us believe that we should be careful not to disparage natural gifts in relation to spiritual gifts in the body of Christ.[15] The same Creator and Spirit gave us both. In fact, many natural gifts can be put to spiritual use once a person is converted and starts using their gifts for the benefit of others in the body of Christ. This is true for leadership gifts, such as teaching or administration. It's also

---

15 The major NT passages on spiritual gifts are Romans 12:3–8, 1 Corinthians 12–14, Ephesians 4:1–16, and 1 Peter 4:7–11.

true for service-related gifts, such as giving or mercy. Similarly, a person with musical gifting will be able to use their gift in a worship context. That said, a person must be *set apart for God's use*—something that is true for them spiritually at conversion but is worked out experientially over time—so they can exercise their spiritual gifts in a God-honoring and beneficial way in the local church. Of course, we're not advocating prematurely appointing a person to a leadership position in the church just because they serve as leaders in their profession.[16]

What are your spiritual gifts? And what spiritual gifts do your children have? Do you know? Have you tried to help them determine what their spiritual gifts are and find appropriate places of ministry where they can exercise those gifts? How should we explore this with our children? What is an appropriate age? We readily concede that we ourselves may not always have done a very good job at that, and probably can improve in this area even now. In fact, it's sometimes hard to know what your gifts are until you start using them (a sort of catch-22). Parents might start by determining and exercising your own gifts in the community of the church. In this way, you'll not only set the example but be better able to help your children as well.

Often the very best way to know what your gifts are is to step out in faith and get involved, or to ask other mature Christians who know you well. What do they perceive your strengths to be? How have they benefited from something you've done, perhaps without your even realizing it? Passing on a legacy of service in the church based on spiritual and natural gifting to your children may involve a *cycle of engagement* because they may not be ready or mature enough

---

16 Qualifications for church leaders can be found in 1 Timothy 3:1–13 and Titus 1:5–9.

spiritually to explore their spiritual gifts at a given point in time.[17] Every child has his or her own experience in life with God and pace of growth in maturity. As parents, we should follow the Spirit's leading in the context of our ongoing relationship with our children.

What About Dating?

Just recently, I was led to ask myself the rather weighty question: How am I preparing my children for marriage? And how am I preparing them for service in the church? When we send our children to college for four years, that college will prepare them for all kinds of things (even things we wish they didn't). Marriage and serving in the church aren't among these and any messages they receive in this area might likely be contrary to what we would hope. And, what to do with that complicated experiment of meeting and getting to know a person that they might marry? That's where we as parents most certainly must come in. Preparing our children for meeting and marrying, as well as serving God, must absolutely be a significant part of *our* vision for parenting.

> *'Somehow, we've embraced the notion that preparing for a vocation takes years of preparation, but marriage can be entered on a whim if we just meet the "right" person!'*

Many of us have embraced the notion that preparing for a vocation takes years of preparation, but marriage can be entered on a whim if we just meet the 'right' person! Thus, many young people enter marriage unprepared, and often experience a rather rude

---

17 Spiritual gifts inventories are often used to help a person identify their spiritual gifts. Ask your pastor to guide you in this, always being careful to take these inventories as guides, not as ultimately determinative.

awakening after the initial honeymoon phase is over (if not before or even during the honeymoon)!

One of the trickiest and most controversial subjects in Christian circles then is the question of dating. How are you supposed to meet your future spouse in a godly way? Should you shop around until you find the best available husband or wife? Is it simply a process of trial and error dating? How do you know whether you and a potential spouse are compatible? And where is God in all of this? One school of thought holds that if the potential partner is a believer, it's up to you to decide. Others contend that God has one person for you to marry and you can trust Him to lead you to that person at His perfect time—so wait. The question is: Can you, and should you, trust God to lead you in this crucial area of life, or can you, and should you, trust yourself to make the right choices and go and find yourself a husband or wife? Or is it somehow a combination between the two ends of the spectrum?

Our Story: Andreas's Version

Well, if you ask a bunch of people, you'll likely get as many different answers as people you ask. That's at least in part because each one of us who is married has our own story to tell of how we met our spouse, and that story has probably shaped our view on the subject. The two of us met in seminary, and believe God has brought us together from different countries and backgrounds to partner in marriage and mission. We first talked on the phone when Margaret called the seminary switchboard, where I worked as an international student, for the whopping pay of $3.35 an hour (but, hey, that's how I met my wife, so I'm not complaining). We talked for what seemed like a rather long time—I was just trying to be helpful in answering Margaret's questions about the school—and at the end of our conversation I told her, 'Why don't you look me up when you come to campus. You shouldn't have any problems finding me—I'm the only Austrian on campus!'

Of course, she didn't look me up, but she did come to my school. Later that fall, I met her again at an open dorm event in the women's dorm. Looking at her photo albums, I found out that her two brothers were both into rock music—remarkable, I thought, for a seminary student at a conservative school, and intriguing since I had played in a band prior to becoming a Christian. Later still, we went on some 'hall dates' together as part of a larger group, playing board games and socializing. At one point, during a winter storm, we went sledding and inner-tubing as a group on campus, on the one rare occasion when the school shut down along with everything else in Columbia, South Carolina. Then the big opportunity came: the formal annual Valentine's banquet. Making sure no one beat me to the punch, I asked Margaret before she left campus for Christmas break—a full two months prior to the banquet! She said yes, but was probably wondering what I was up to. Sure enough, someone else asked her not too long after I did, so I'm so glad I didn't take any chances!

In any case, the banquet went well (we still have a picture to prove it), and in the following weeks we went on some long walks and had some in-depth conversations about what it meant for each of us to follow Christ and what each of our plans were for the future. These conversations helped for us to remove some potential obstacles, such as that I wondered if Margaret was headed for the mission field in Africa (I had no such designs). Fortunately, I discovered that she simply went to church with friends who were missionaries to Africa without necessarily feeling called to go there herself. In any case, to make a long story short, I visited her in her home country of Canada that summer, and I later invited her to join me on a trip to my home town of Vienna, Austria the following Christmas.

We enjoyed getting to know each other over the period of about a year, bonding over the fact that both of us were from a culture other than the United States, and at some point during that year (I think it was that summer when I visited in Canada) I asked Margaret if she wanted to seriously pursue a relationship with me. She said yes! A little over a year after our first date, I asked Margaret to marry me on a day trip to Charleston, South Carolina. We went to church that Sunday morning and afterwards sat down to talk on a white park bench near the church. I was just about to pull out the ring from my pocket with my sweaty fingers as Margaret, perhaps nervous and sensing something was about to happen, suddenly jumped up and said, 'Let's go and get some lunch.' Slightly startled, I recovered and complied.

It took several hours before the next opportune time presented itself for me to ask Margaret to marry me, at Boone Hall Plantation near a pond under a big, shady tree. This time I took no chances and pulled out the ring right away. 'Will you marry me?' I asked, and with only a moment's hesitation she said, 'Yes.' The drive home that evening was exhilarating, as we talked about a wedding date, telling our parents, and making plans for our future together. Not quite nine months later we were married in Toronto, Canada, on a frosty winter day complete with a light dusting of snow. In short, that's how God brought the two of us together. At least, that's my side of the story!

Our Story: Margaret's Version
How did I meet my husband? I was in my apartment one Sunday afternoon, reviewing the list of potential seminaries I

could go to, and decided to call Columbia Bible College and Seminary. Andreas answered the phone. He was a foreign student on an international visa who was only permitted to work for income on campus. It was a quiet afternoon for both of us, so Andreas took time to talk to me about the seminary. I had sent requests for information to several schools but was interested in Columbia because of what they identified as their 'whole life training' approach to education. Since I came from a non-Christian home and was craving mentoring, this offer was something I wanted to pursue. At the end of the conversation, Andreas told me to look him up when I got to campus, saying, 'I'm the only Austrian on campus.'

I decided to go to Columbia, but didn't follow up on the conversation with Andreas as it didn't remain very prominent in my mind. A few months later, there was an open house in our dorm for the male student's dorm to visit, and Andreas stopped by my room. Again, this was incidental on his part, I thought, and didn't remain very prominent in my mind. He asked me questions about my family and brothers but I didn't consider any of it remarkable. Later, during a rare snow day in Columbia, SC, House 14 on campus hosted a game night; I loved that living situation on campus, as it was in a real house, and took the opportunity to fellowship there with other students. I later remember seeing a picture of this event where I sat beside Andreas, playing a game at a table there. Otherwise I may not have even remembered he was there. He was very quiet. That same evening, the group went inner-tubing, and I remember interacting very slightly with Andreas.

As the Valentine's Day banquet rose on the horizon, I decided I would just agree to go with the first person who asked me (if anyone did ask me!). I didn't have a preference on any one person, so was completely open to the Lord's leading. Before I went home to Canada for Christmas, at least six weeks before the banquet, Andreas came up and asked me to go to the banquet with him. I agreed. The night of the banquet, after the meal, we went for a long walk to the 'Point' at the end of the road where the house of the president of the college was located. Students were welcome to come sit on the swing in the grassy area there and to relax and pray, so we took advantage of this and talked for a while, and later Andreas walked me back to my dorm. No physical displays of affection were permitted at the school prior to engagement and we complied.

In the months that followed, Andreas occasionally asked me to go off campus for cinnamon rolls at Cinnabon or for dinner. Once, at a Ruby Tuesday restaurant, we ordered coffee and an apple cobbler to split, but the waitress brought just one plate, which led to an awkward moment, because I really didn't want to share a dessert with Andreas at that point (too intimate!). I had barely just met him! We kept going for occasional walks and were both busy studying. Cell phones were not a public commodity at the time, so when Andreas wanted to call, he rang the dorm, and whoever answered the phone in the long hall would come find me to answer the call. On occasion, it was I who initiated and suggested going for a walk. I enjoyed his company and walking, too! We talked a lot about discipleship and our respective cultural backgrounds. We gradually started spending more and more time together, though I can't remember at what point we considered ourselves to be dating. I wasn't interested in anyone else at that time and was spending time with just Andreas getting to know him.

Later that spring, I decided to stay in school for a second year, since I had barely scratched the surface in terms of the spiritual knowledge I felt I needed to gain for myself.

My purpose for going to seminary was to be grounded in the Word and to prepare for a life of ministry, and one year was barely getting me there. The first summer, I went back to Canada, worked as a nurse, and Andreas came up to visit, staying with a couple I knew from church and college ministry at McMaster University. I didn't exactly know how I felt about the relationship in terms of long-term commitment, so Andreas was obviously disappointed when he realized that. He came to attention and asked me to make up my mind. I felt pressed to make a choice and decided that I wanted to continue to pursue the relationship. The entire year prior to marriage we discussed a lot of details about our background. It was a very difficult year, and many times I was discouraged. We disagreed quite a bit about issues related to personal holiness, addressing such questions as which movies we would prefer to watch (or avoid); but Andreas was very honest, and was working out his own holiness and life before the Lord. He had an obvious love for the Lord and was extremely knowledgable about God's Word, which attracted me to him. Since we both had only been believers for about four years when we met, we were both essentially just beginning of our journey with Christ.

The following Christmas Andreas invited me to join him to travel to Vienna, Austria. I met his mother and sister. We took part in many interesting and fun Austrian traditions including lit candles on the tree (only put up just the day before Christmas), celebrating on the evening of the 24th, and a special meal on St. Stephen's Day (deer!) at Uncle Hermann's house. We had coffee and cake with Tante Mina at her sophisticated home on a crisp white linen-covered coffee table. We even went to Mass with his family at St. Stephen's Chapel in Vienna, though Andreas had left the Catholic Church when he became a believer. We also attended the

Vienna International Chapel—the church Andreas had gone to as a new believer—and met some missionaries he had known before leaving Austria to go to seminary.

As we came back from the trip, there were a lot of expectations. 'So what happened? No ring? Is everything OK?' My response was, 'Well, Andreas just wanted me to meet his family, since he realized that with him being from another country this would be a big step for everyone. He wanted me to know what I might be getting myself into if we marry.' Andreas was also trying to honor his family, especially his mother, by introducing me to her and treating her with respect. We went back to a hard semester of studying for me, and grading papers and teaching his first class in the evenings for Andreas. I attended the first course Andreas taught on Old Testament survey! It was good for the first class he ever taught.

Then, in March, Andreas asked me to go on a day trip to Charleston, South Carolina. We went to the centrally located St. Michael's Anglican Church for the Sunday morning service, and afterwards sat on a bench near the church to talk for a few minutes. I didn't realize that Andreas had been looking for an opportunity to ask me to marry him and had been ready to do so when I abruptly stood up and said, 'Let's go.' Later that afternoon, we visited Boone Hall Plantation, walked around the property on the grassy back area beside a pond. I noticed that Andreas was kind of quiet, and then stopped, and he asked me, 'What would you say if I were to ask you to marry me?' I said, 'Well, I would say yes.' Then Andreas said, 'So *will* you marry me?' I said yes. It was already late afternoon and about to get dark, so we got into our car and drove back to Columbia, spending the ride back talking about telling others about our engagement and beginning plans for our wedding.

The Ultimate Matchmaker

It won't surprise you that we believe that God does indeed bring two people, a man and a woman, together to lead them into a relationship so they become husband and wife. God is the ultimate 'Matchmaker'! The book of Proverbs says that 'He who finds a wife finds what is good and receives favor from the LORD.'[18] As the God of providence, the God who sovereignly directs the affairs of men—and women, too— cares for every intimate detail of our lives, much more so about whom we will marry. As Peter writes in his first epistle, 'Cast all your anxiety on him, because he cares for you.'[19] So what does it mean to trust God in this area of our lives? It means that we resist the urge to take matters into our own hands as parents, or as the one seeking God in this matter. We don't encourage manipulating others by flirting or aggressive behavior. Young men take appropriate Spirit-led initiative, while young women joyfully respond—or graciously resist— as they sense the Lord's leading (or lack thereof).

Clearly, the area of male-female relationships including a possible marriage relationship is too serious a matter to take out of God's hands into our own. We need to be careful to find the appropriate and responsible balance of influence in our children's lives in this area. Often the wisdom of parents is given insufficient weight while, at

> 'Young men take appropriate Spirit-led initiative, while young women joyfully respond—or graciously resist—as they sense the Lord's leading (or lack thereof).'

least in our experience, peers and even pastors (doubtless with good intentions) tend to take over. Cooperation and coordi-

18 Proverbs 18:22.

19 1 Peter 5:7.

nation between parents and pastors, however, can be helpful here. So do be in touch with the college pastor if there is one. Instructing our children in this area of life involves helping them realize that God knows the end from the beginning; He will do what He knows is best.

At the same time, as in education, we as parents should take our responsibility seriously to guide our children in this very important matter. It seems vital to begin training and guiding them relatively early to help boys not to 'burn' with passion and turn to pornography because they are not married. Similarly, if girls wait too long to get married, they may be tempted to settle for a husband who is not a strong Christian partly out of loneliness. Remaining single for long may engender too much independence. The same goes for young men as well. The longer they wait, the more difficult it may be for either to be flexible and open to accommodate another person in their life.[20]

We also need to be ready to discuss that in some rare cases, God may call a man or woman to remain unmarried so they can serve Him without being distracted by family responsibilities. But be clear that God will lead this way normally only if He gives them the gift ('charisma') of singleness (or celibacy) as mentioned before. If your child shudders at the thought that they may have such a gift, chances are they don't! As a matter of fact, you can encourage them that from the beginning God created man and woman for each other for companionship and fruitfulness on purpose! It follows that God intends that most people marry.

In any case, we shouldn't put God in a box because there are many ways in which He can bring two people together. There are more stories that are unique, including one from

---

20 Thanks to Nancy Finneran for sharing the helpful insights contained in this paragraph.

our current pastor who said he knew the first time he met his future wife that they were meant for each other—and told her so! As if that wasn't amazing enough, his future wife told him she agreed! Obviously, that's probably not going to be the norm, but it illustrates that there are many ways in which God may bring two people together and confirm His leading in their lives.

Finding a Spouse: Dating or Friendship?

The Bible says that 'it is not good for man to be alone.'[21] We believe that the same principle holds true for women, too. We were made for companionship, not aloneness, and can all attest to the fact that loneliness is a scourge, not a blessing. So, how should we look for a potential partner to share life with? Should Christians date? And if so, how?[22] Or is what people sometimes label 'courtship' a better way to go?[23] The difference between these approaches is that in *dating* a man and a woman spend time together exclusively for a period to determine whether they're meant to get married, while in *courtship* a commitment is made at the outset that a couple

---

21 Genesis 2:18.

22 A classic critique of dating is Joshua Harris, *I Kissed Dating Goodbye* (Colorado Springs: Multnomah, 2003). See also Richard D. Phillips and Sharon L. Phillips, *Holding Hands, Holding Hearts: Recovering a Biblical View of Christian Dating* (Phillipsburg, NJ: P&R, 2006), who point out that the Bible says nothing about 'dating' and that 'dating is essentially a twentieth-century invention' (p. 12). And yet, the authors argue, you can't simply 'kiss [dating] goodbye' (p. 12, alluding to Harris's book?); rather, they 'take the biblical principles of a healthy marriage and work backwards toward a healthy dating relationship' (p. 13), which involves commitment, intimacy, and interdependence (pp. 31–36). Like our book *God's Design for Man and Woman*, the authors move from creation to the Fall and redemption, through which a couple can move from manipulation to ministry (pp. 58–63).

23 Douglas Wilson, *Her Hand in Marriage: Biblical Courtship in the Modern World* (Moscow, ID: Canon, 1997).

is pursuing the likelihood of marriage, having previously known each other in a larger social context such as church, college, family relationship, or friendship groups.

What are the pros and cons of dating versus alternate approaches? Dating, especially at an early age, usually involves long periods of time spent together to determine compatibility. Authors Richard and Sharon Philips sketch the picture of dating essentially as follows:

> If marriage is in the picture at all, then dating is a tryout for a potential partner. The idea is to start living as if you were married and see how things go. If one isn't finding fulfillment in the other person, then you can simply break up and move on. It's not much different from finding the right pair of shoes. At least you can have some fun along the way, or so it goes.[24]

There may be a certain amount of caricature in this description, as not all would agree that in dating people 'start living as if [they] were married,' but you get the picture. There may be a certain trial-and-error component in the process involved as well, as one would assume (though this is not necessarily an accurate assumption) that people gradually get smarter and learn what they need in another person to be fulfilled, until— so the theory goes—they eventually find 'The One.'

Our concern, however, is that there's an important sense in which moving toward marriage is *unlike* shopping for shoes or some other item. The reason for this is that men and women are *people*, with feelings and personalities, not inanimate objects! Also, the kind of extended time spent exclusively on dates may render young people vulnerable to greater intimacy than appropriate and render them vulnerable to sexual temptation when they aren't yet ready for marriage; as

---

24 Phillips and Phillips, *Holding Hands, Holding Hearts*, 14.

a result, one or both may get hurt in the process. Often much time and emotional energy are spent (wasted) that could have been used in the service of God. Other important and healthy relationships often become marginalized early, far before a sole commitment is even necessary. Dating, or serial dating, may also have the potential of developing a relational habit of transience rather than that of one-person permanence, and make it more difficult for a person eventually to settle down. And people—especially young women—may feel used or even used up in the process. You get the picture—we're not huge fans of unbridled dating!

The bottom line is that care and prayer should be taken in the process of getting to know the opposite sex. To counteract the above-mentioned potential negative entailments of dating, some, as mentioned, favor an approach called 'courtship.' Yet this may be a bit reactionary and cause the pendulum to swing too far to the other extreme, from too flippant and casual an approach to one that gets too serious too soon. In fact, the courtship approach is uncomfortable for some because at times it requires young men to make a commitment to a woman (and vice versa) usually before he (and she) is ready or may not even know each other very well. Personally, we encourage what you might call a 'friendship' approach which allows young adults time to get to know each other in larger and smaller group settings, hopefully in wholesome fellowship and in serving the Lord in local church ministry contexts amongst other things. If God leads a couple to recognize the potential for a special relationship beyond the friendship level, they may choose to go deeper, depending also on their age and stage in life. This cautious approach is helpful because it gives the opportunity for people to become acquainted without any pressure being

	Approach	Brief Description
1	Dating	Spending time together exclusively for a certain amount of time to enjoy the opposite sex, not always with the purpose of finding a marriage partner. Serial dating may ensue with several or many people, with or without the purpose of finding a marriage partner.
2	Courtship	Commitment at the outset of spending time together (usually with parents' permission) that the couple is pursuing marriage. Time together also involves accountability of an outside party.
3	Friend-ship	Young people get to know each other in larger and smaller group settings (or other informal ways) to form friendships before committing to a purposeful (likely to get married) but still exploratory relationship.

Figure 6: Three Approaches to Finding a Life Partner

placed on either person to commit before they know what they're getting themselves into.

For reasons such as these, therefore, it likely seems best to proceed slowly until there's a growing and clear conviction that God may be at work. Be patient for God to bring someone across your path at the right time when both are ready to pursue a committed relationship. At that point, a young man may choose to initiate a relationship with a young woman when both are getting close to being ready for marriage, which—depending on circumstances, such as their age and the girl's parents' receptivity—may involve the young man's securing her father's permission to do so.

The following list of characteristics of a 'redeemed man'— that is, a Christian young man who seeks to put God first in his pursuit of a healthy relationship with a young lady— is inspired by a similar list in Richard and Sharon Phillips's *Holding Hands, Holding Hearts*:[25]

- Accept responsibility to lead the relationship in a godly direction, including setting proper boundaries to guard against sexual sin; treat her as a precious sister in Christ.
- Resolve to love her in a self-sacrificing, Christlike way that puts her interests above your own; take interest in her, ask her questions, and do the kinds of things she likes to do.
- Initiate honest conversation about the relationship and do not ignore her desires, feelings, or cautions; listen to her heart.
- Be a spiritual leader and share with her insights from God's Word; make it your goal that she will be spiritually stronger rather than weaker because of your relationship.

---

25 Ibid., 77–78.

- Pray for her in any areas of weakness; if you don't want to pursue the relationship any further, tell her so honestly and kindly.

The equivalent list for a 'redeemed woman' would look something like this:[26]

- Permit him to initiate the relationship; you can encourage him and respond to him, even help him, but don't manipulate or take over.
- Do the opposite—that is, discourage the relationship—if you don't want to pursue it!
- Speak well of him and of the relationship to his face and to your friends.
- Show interest in the things he enjoys and be responsive to his questions and initiatives if and as appropriate.
- Recognize the possibility of sexual temptation and dress and act in a modest and godly way that will not unnecessarily tempt him; don't use your physical attributes to win him over.
- Encourage him in his spiritual life (my wife excelled in this prior to our engagement; she would often give me cards of encouragement, often with Bible verses).
- Treat him as a brother in Christ; if you don't see the relationship continuing, tell him so kindly and graciously.

Please feel free to share these lists with your teenager and college-age children. Also, encourage them to make the most of the time when they're not yet married.[27] God is molding

---

26 Ibid., 85–87. On what women can do to encourage marriage, see Candice Watters, *Get Married: What Women Can Do to Help It Happen* (Chicago: Moody, 2008).

27 This is the premise of Marshall Segal, *Not Yet Married: The Pursuit of Joy in Singleness and Dating* (Wheaton: Crossway, 2017).

and shaping them into the person He wants them to be. May God be glorified and may young women especially be protected in this delicate area of our lives. As in other areas, we should trust God to guide us, and He certainly will. As parents, we should impress on our children their need for wisdom and discernment in choosing a life partner. We should let them know that we respect their right to choose their own life partner but that we're available to give input whenever they're open to it and provide support whenever it's needed. We could also communicate that while the choice of a spouse is ultimately their decision, it does have obvious implications for the entire family.

On the one hand, we shouldn't uphold standards that are so high that no earthly being could ever attain to it—especially in their late teens or early twenties! On the other hand, we shouldn't hesitate to express concerns and reservations if they're well founded, and hopefully our children will listen. If they believe that we have their best interests at heart, and that we want them to be happy, they'll realize that we're not trying to be obstructionist but rather draw on decades of life experience from which they can benefit. If parents have been relational all along, being involved in this process won't be awkward but normal. Parental involvement is especially important with girls who, prior to marriage, would continue to benefit from the guidance and protection of their father.

Practical Tips

Our main advice for our children in seeking a spouse is to pray for the person God has designed for them and to discern a prospective life partner first by the love he has for *God* and then by the love he has for *them*. Also, as mentioned, build

> 'A strong friendship is a lasting foundation for a strong marriage.'

solid *friendships*—even in marriage, a strong friendship is a lasting foundation for a strong marriage. In the meantime, help them to be patient and to keep pursuing that to which God has called them in terms of education and vocational preparation, whether male or female. Entering too quickly into a relationship from a point of desperation—not just need—not only has some of the above-mentioned drawbacks but may render one unduly dependent on others and vulnerable to be taken advantage of.

As you pray for them and, as appropriate, advise them and provide a sounding board, help them to find someone who is compatible. By 'compatible' we mean *not* that they're the same but that they complement each other well. One may have a rather quiet personality and the other may be outgoing. In terms of age, calling, mission, interests, and even socio-economic and cultural background, it's likely beneficial to have some similarities of background and more importantly, calling. In any case, it's important to work through any differences and expectations for life, marriage, and family to avoid later difficulties in the context of lifelong commitment. It would be easy to dismiss these things when you are 'in love,' but the honeymoon won't last forever.

Couples could also use a more detailed 'birds and bees' talk just prior to marriage. It seems that few young couples receive this talk. We think this may be because usually those who do premarital counseling are older and wiser but often don't remember the challenges they might have had with intimacy in the very beginning of marriage. In fact, virtually *every* couple or friend we've talked to about this said that this topic wasn't covered thoroughly enough in premarital counseling, or even by their parents, and for many their early marriage relationship was challenging as a result. If parents don't remember much about their own honeymoon, they could facilitate a talk between their engaged adult child and a young couple their son or daughter knows and trusts.

So much more could be said about this subject, but for now these few reflections must suffice.[28]

Parenting Is Never Done

One more thing: If you think that parenting is over when you send your children off to college or even when they marry, think again! We've found the opposite to be the case. It's exactly when you let your children go and they experience the freedom that comes with college life that they often realize that they need and desire parental and others' input, so they can make good decisions in a variety of areas. Few young people are fully prepared for everything when they leave for college despite your best efforts to equip them for life. They may contact you and want to talk to you about struggles in relationships, ask for your help in developing study skills, or want you to give advice on that first job interview or subsequent ones. This, of course, presupposes that you have cultivated the kind of relationship with them while they were at home that engendered trust and conveyed to them a sense that you love them in the way very few others do or ever will.

So, don't look at parenting as something that will end when your kids go off to college or at some other time. We don't even have space here to discuss the joys of being grandparents. That would clearly take another book (not for us to write; we're not grandparents yet!). We mean that if you're a father or mother, you'll always be a father or mother. The nature of your relationship with your children will change over time, and will most likely turn into a close friendship, if

---

28 For additional food for thought, see 'Part Two: Biblical Wisdom for Dating and Relationships,' in Phillips and Phillips, *Holding Hands, Holding Hearts*, 89–177.

all goes well. But there'll always be a sense in which you can provide guidance and share your life experience with the next generation. In fact, that's why we wrote this book.

The Bottom Line

As responsible parents who nurture and equip their children with perspective and purpose along the entire life cycle of parenting, one of our greatest joys and challenges is to equip our children for their mission in life. In doing so, a solid grasp of the mission of God as conveyed in the biblical storyline will be indispensable. Based on understanding the four movements in the divine symphony of creating and redeeming a people for God, we'll be able to assist our children in finding their mission and purpose in life, including their service and vocation in the local church. Be a perceptive observer and a good listener of your children. Every child is different and individually fashioned by God with unique gifts and a tailor-made calling.

> *'Don't look at parenting as something that will end when your kids go off to college or at some other time.'*

The mystery is that we have a sovereign, transcendent God who is at the same time concerned for every detail of our lives (including our marriage partner!).

What makes things more intriguing and at times more perplexing is that God normally reveals His will for us as part of a process rather than all at once. This requires many small steps of obedience and responses along the way. We must follow Him in what He has already revealed to us or we can't expect Him to reveal what He next wants us to do in the future. We must keep in step with God as we walk with Him through life. In the Bible, we read about believers who 'walked with God' for dozens and in some cases even hundreds of years.[29] Can you image the intimacy that comes from living life closely aligned with another person? Those of us who have been married for twenty or more years can appreciate the transformative power and potential of this kind of union. As Jesus memorably put it,

> I am the vine; you are the branches. Whoever abides in me and I in him, he it is that bears much fruit, for apart from me you can do nothing… If you abide in me, and my words abide in you, ask whatever you wish, and it will be done for you. By this my Father is glorified, that you bear much fruit and so prove to be my disciples.[30]

May we walk closely with Him and with each other throughout our parenting journey, and may we inspire our children to do the same.

What's Next?

1. Considering what was said about finding our mission in view of God's mission, is there anything you need to change regarding your perspective on your role as a parent in your child's life? If so, what kinds of changes do you need to make?

2. Have you identified your own God-given mission in life? If so, are you modeling this God-given mission in front of your children? What is your mission in life, and how do you know?

3. What, would you say, is your children's mission in life, one by one? How much progress have you and they made in discovering God's purpose for their lives?

---

29 E.g., Enoch in the book of Genesis, who was taken up when he was 365 years old (Genesis 5:24).

30 John 15:5, 7–8.

Conclusion

We're so grateful you joined us on this journey toward realistic, relational, and responsible parenting. We know that there are many unique challenges that you'll have to navigate on your own in your context. What we've attempted to provide in this book is a biblical-theological framework for being the kinds of parents God intends us to be, with some actionable information. In the preceding pages, we've covered quite a bit of ground in moving through the various component parts of this framework. In so doing, we've sought to supply you with essential planks in the house we've tried to build, designed to help you in your God-given joy and privilege of equipping your children for life.

Whether you're parents already or aspiring to be parents or better parents, we hope this book has inspired you to excel in this pursuit, with God's help and for His glory. We hope that reading this book has given you *hope*—parenting has its challenges, but it has even greater rewards. We've written this book in the conviction that by God's grace and in

His strength, we can love, nurture, and equip our children for the life and the mission God has for them. Properly conceived, parenting should focus *neither* on the parents *nor* the children; rather, we should all humble ourselves under the mighty hand of God and together strive to be, and become, the people He has created us to be. He is the Perfect Parent—our Heavenly Father, 'from whom every family in heaven and on earth is named.'[1]

Again, thank you for joining us on this journey. Continue to reflect on the Bible verses we suggested and to ponder the thoughts, experiences, and insights we shared in this book. We're praying for you, our fellow parents, especially younger parents. Keep up the parenting journey in the Lord! It is so important! We love you and your family and would love to hear from you. Contact us at www.biblicalfoundations.org and leave your comment or question. We'll respond to you there!

> Now to Him who is able to do far more abundantly beyond all that we ask or think, according to the power that works within us, to Him be the glory in the church and in Christ Jesus to all generations forever and ever. Amen.[2]

---

1   Ephesians 3:15.

2   Ephesians 3:20–21 (NASB).

Recommended Resources[1]

Andreas Köstenberger. *Excellence: The Character of God and the Pursuit of Scholarly Virtue.* Wheaton: Crossway, 2011.

Andreas Köstenberger with David Jones. *God, Marriage, and Family: Rebuilding the Biblical Foundation.* Second edition. Wheaton: Crossway, 2010. Abridged as *Marriage and the Family: Biblical Essentials.* Wheaton: Crossway, 2012.

Andreas and Margaret Köstenberger. *God's Design for Man and Woman: A Biblical-Theological Survey.* Wheaton: Crossway, 2014. Also available in course format at www. biblemesh.com and www.biblicalfoundations.org: *God's Design for Man and Woman* (full course), *Man and Woman: Biblical Essentials* (abridged course).

Andy Crouch. *The Tech-Wise Family: Everyday Steps for Putting Technology in Its Proper Place.* Grand Rapids: Baker, 2017.

---

1 In addition to the Bible!

Brent Crowe. *Chasing Elephants: Wrestling with the Gray Areas of Life*. Colorado Springs: NavPress, 2010.

C. J. Mahaney. *Humility: True Greatness*. Sisters, OR: Multnomah, 2005.

C. J. Mahaney, editor. *Worldliness: Resisting the Seduction of a Fallen World*. Wheaton: Crossway, 2008.

Candice Watters. *Get Married: What Women Can Do to Help It Happen*. Chicago: Moody, 2008.

Carolyn Mahaney and Nicole Mahaney Whitacre. *Girl Talk: Mother-Daughter Conversations on Biblical Womanhood*. Wheaton: Crossway, 2005.

Dennis and Barbara Rainey. *Passport2Purity*. Little Rock, AR: FamilyLife, 2012.

Dennis and Barbara Rainey and others. *Passport2Identity for Young Men. Passport2Identity for Young Women*. Little Rock, AR: FamilyLife, 2016.

Dennis Rainey. *Stepping Up: A Call to Courageous Manhood*. Little Rock, AR: FamilyLife, 2011.

Donald Whitney. *Family Worship*. Wheaton: Crossway, 2016.

Donald Whitney. *Spiritual Disciplines for the Christian Life*. Revised edition. Colorado Springs: Nav Press, 2014.

Gary Chapman with Shannon Warden. *Things I Wish I'd Known Before We Became Parents*. Chicago: Northfield, 2016.

Ginger Plowman Hubbard. *'Don't Make Me Count to Three!' A Mom's Look at Heart-Oriented Discipline*. Wapwallopen, PA: Shepherd, 2004.

Ginger Hubbard. *Wise Words for Moms*. Wapwallopen, PA: Shepherd, 2001.

Gloria Furman. *Glimpses of Grace: Treasuring the Gospel in Your Home*. Wheaton: Crossway, 2013.

Gloria Furman. *Missional Motherhood: The Everyday Ministry of Motherhood in the Grand Plan of God*. Wheaton: Crossway, 2016.

Gloria Furman. *Treasuring Christ When Your Hands Are Full: Gospel Meditations for Busy Moms*. Wheaton: Crossway, 2014.

Harriet Connor. *Big Picture Parents: Ancient Wisdom for Modern Life*. Eugene, OR: Wipf & Stock, 2017.

Jen Wilkin. *Women of the Word: How to Study the Bible with Both Our Hearts and Our Minds*. Wheaton: Crossway, 2014.

Joshua Harris. *I Kissed Dating Goodbye: A New Attitude toward Romance and Relationships*. Updated edition. Colorado Springs: Multnomah, 2003.

Joshua Harris. *Sex Is Not the Problem (Lust Is): Sexual Purity in a Lust-Saturated World*. Colorado Springs: Multnomah, 2005.

Justin Buchanan. *Guys and Lies: Nine Lies the Enemy Tells Young Men*. Raleigh, NC: Bay Press, 2011.

Ken Sande, with Tom Raabe. *Peacemaking for Families: A Biblical Guide to Managing Conflict in Your Home*. Wheaton: Tyndale, 2002.

Kent Hughes. *Disciplines of a Godly Young Man*. Wheaton: Crossway, 2012.

Leighann McCoy. *Spiritual Warfare for Your Family: What You Need to Know to Protect Your Children*. Minneapolis: Bethany House, 2016.

Marshall Segal. *Not Yet Married: The Pursuit of Joy in Singleness and Dating*. Wheaton: Crossway, 2017.

Mary A. Kassian. *Girls Gone Wise in a World Gone Wild.* Chicago: Moody, 2010.

Nancy Leigh DeMoss and Dannah Gresh. *Lies Young Women Believe and the Truth That Sets Them Free.* Chicago: Moody, 2008.

Paul David Tripp. *Age of Opportunity: A Biblical Guide to Parenting Teens.* Second edition. Phillipsburg, NJ: P&R, 2001.

Paul David Tripp. *Parenting: 14 Gospel Principles That Can Radically Change Your Family.* Wheaton: Crossway, 2016.

Rachel Jankovic. *Loving the Little Years: Motherhood in the Trenches.* Moscow, ID: Canon, 2010.

Ray Comfort. *How to Bring Your Children to Christ … & Keep Them There: Avoiding the Tragedy of False Conversion.* Bartlesville, OK: Genesis, 2003.

Richard D. Phillips. *The Masculine Mandate: God's Calling to Men.* Sanford, FL: Reformation Trust, 2010.

Richard and Sharon Phillips. *Holding Hands, Holding Hearts: Recovering a Biblical View of Christian Dating.* Phillipsburg, NJ: P&R, 2006.

Sally Clarkson. *The Mission of Motherhood: Touching Your Child's Heart for Eternity.* Colorado Springs: Waterbrook, 2003.

Steve and Candice Watters. *Start Your Family: Inspiration for Having Babies.* Chicago: Moody, 2009.

Susan Wise Bauer and Jessie Wise. *The Well-Trained Mind: A Guide to Classical Education at Home.* 4th edition. New York/London: W. W. Norton & Co., 2016.

Susan Wise Bauer. *The Story of the World: History for the Classical Child.* 4 vols. Charles City, VA: Peace Hill Press, 2003–2006.

Tedd Tripp. *Shepherding a Child's Heart.* Revised and updated edition. Wapwallopen, PA: Shepherd, 1995.

www.biblicalfoundations.org *This website features accessible articles, blogs, videos, and other resources on topics such as apologetics, biblical interpretation, biblical theology, Jesus, Christmas, and Easter, marriage and family, missions and discipleship, and issues of concern to women.*

General Index

Scripture Index

Also available from Christian Focus...

| LUKE |

GEOFF GLEASON

A Family Worship Guide to Luke

Geoff Gleason

This new series of Bible studies for the family is written for the parent in the pew. Each volume serves as an aid to fathers and mothers as they seek to lead their families in daily worship together. The lessons review the main point of the passage under consideration, offer suggested discussion points for children of a variety of ages, suggest songs to broaden the family's song repertoire, and identify items of prayer.

'This guide offers the head of a household a concise analysis of the day's reading from Luke that he can review in two minutes, helpful guidelines for age-appropriate discussions, a suggested psalm or hymn to sing, and a starting point for family prayer. What a help and what a blessing!'

Joel R. Beeke
President of Puritan Reformed Theological Seminary,
Grand Rapids, Michigan

'The realities of practicing family worship often make the benefits seem distant or even inaccessible. We aren't sure what to say about a passage, how to apply the text in an age-appropriate way, or even what to pray. Geoff Gleason gently and helpfully takes the reader by the hand and simplifies the practice of family worship.'

Jason Helopoulos
Associate Pastor, University Reformed Church,
East Lansing, Michigan

ISBN 978-1-5271-0040-4

THE ENVY OF *Eve*

FINDING CONTENTMENT IN A COVETOUS WORLD

MELISSA B. KRUGER

The Envy of Eve
Finding Contentment in a Covetous World
Melissa B. Kruger

What's truly at the heart of our desires? The Envy of Eve guides readers to understand how desires grow into covetousness and what happens when this sin takes power in our hearts. Covetousness chokes out the fruit of the Spirit in our lives, allowing discontentment to bloom. The key to overcoming is to get to the root of our problem: unbelief-a mistrust of God's sovereignty and goodness. An ideal resource for deeper study or group discussion.

'I commend this fine, new book...with a prayer that we all read and follow her Biblical counsel to fully understand the condition we are in and flee quickly to the One who truly satisfies our deepest longings and our true desires.'

Michael A. Milton
President and Senior Fellow at D. James Kennedy
Institute for Christianity and Culture

'... the author loves Christ, shares her struggles honestly and writes with a sincere desire to encourage her sisters in Christ.'

New Horizons Magazine

ISBN 978-1-8455-0775-6

JOHN A. HUFFMAN, JR

the family

HOW TO BUILD AN AUTHENTIC, LOVING HOME

you want

The Family You Want
How to Build an Authentic, Loving Home
John Huffman

In an age of broken homes and disintegrating family structures, John Huffman investigates the real issues at stake in the family and helps you to live in the best family that you are able to have. John takes us through the issues associated with work, spirituality, emotions, children, parenting, the extended family, divorce, sex, and marriage. With chapters entitled 'What Jesus can do for your family' and 'Why work should be your fourth priority' the book is an enjoyable and easy read, with a much-needed message. John's advice is practical and comes with solid biblical foundations; it is precisely what is needed for the Families of the 21st Century.

'a biblically and faith-based, pragmatic resource for families and for those of us who work with families. He is realistic and honest, and provides a healthy map for daily living.'

Ralph H Earle
Former President of American Association of Marriage and Family Counsellors

'I highly recommend it, for our family relationships can be the cause both of the highest earthly joy, and also the deepest pain. John Huffman has written a book that is both biblical and practical; with high ideals but a realistic understanding that we all struggle with this most important of human relations.'

Leighton Ford
President, Leighton Ford Ministries, Charlotte, North Carolina

ISBN 978-1-8579-2933-1

Christian Focus Publications

Our mission statement –

STAYING FAITHFUL

In dependence upon God we seek to impact the world through literature faithful to His infallible Word, the Bible. Our aim is to ensure that the Lord Jesus Christ is presented as the only hope to obtain forgiveness of sin, live a useful life and look forward to heaven with Him.

Our Books are published in four imprints:

CHRISTIAN FOCUS

popular works including biographies, commentaries, basic doctrine and Christian living.

CHRISTIAN HERITAGE

books representing some of the best material from the rich heritage of the church.

MENTOR

books written at a level suitable for Bible College and seminary students, pastors, and other serious readers. The imprint includes commentaries, doctrinal studies, examination of current issues and church history.

CF4•K

children's books for quality Bible teaching and for all age groups: Sunday school curriculum, puzzle and activity books; personal and family devotional titles, biographies and inspirational stories – Because you are never too young to know Jesus!

Christian Focus Publications Ltd,
Geanies House, Fearn, Ross-shire,
IV20 1TW, Scotland, United Kingdom.
www.christianfocus.com

4/19